I0437989

THE CHILDREN OF JOB
BOOK ONE

The Children of Job

Book One

Cynthia Jacobs

Copyright © 2009 by Cynthia Jacobs.

Library of Congress Control Number:		2009900408
ISBN:	Hardcover	978-1-4415-0364-0
	Softcover	978-1-4415-0363-3

All rights reserved. No part of this book may be reproduced or transmitted
in any form or by any means, electronic or mechanical, including photocopying,
recording, or by any information storage and retrieval system,
without permission in writing from the copyright owner.

This book was printed in the United States of America.

To order additional copies of this book, contact:
Xlibris Corporation
1-888-795-4274
www.Xlibris.com
Orders@Xlibris.com
53743

CONTENTS

Edited by Linda Hilbert

DEDICATION

In memory of Crystal Hammonds, the daughter of my dearest friends Miranda and TR Hammonds. Crystal was born February 13, 1991 and died suddenly of Leukemia on May 4, 2001. Crystal was truly an Angel who walked among us for a short while. We will always love you.

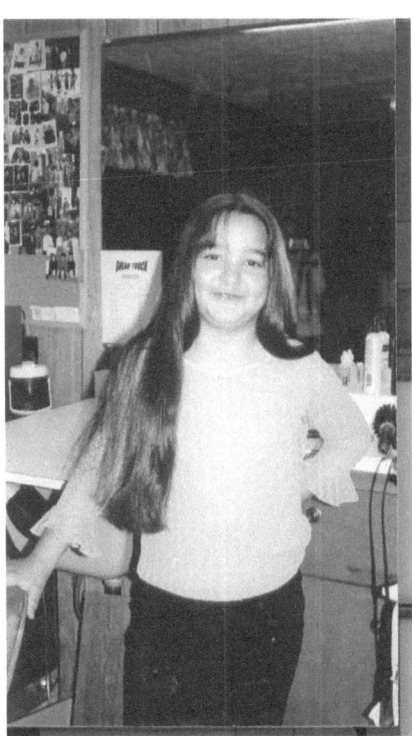

FORWARD

Cynthia Jacobs does a nice job of inviting the reader to step into the everyday family life of a young Lumbee Indian farm boy named Larry, during the Great Depression era. Ms. Jacobs' book provides chapters about survival of a Lumbee Indian family located in southeastern North Carolina, Robeson County. Because of the books historical nature, it is a book that can be added to the Native American Literature category.

Many Native Americans and Indigenous people recall reading books in school like "Dick and Jean". With a surge of Native American writers like Ms Jacobs, who is a Lumbee Indian; such books give a perspective about tribal and Indigenous ways of life. As these types of Indian literature emerge from eastern Native writers, the repertoire of diversity and selections of Native stories are enhanced. As Vine Deloria once said, it is important for Natives to tell their own stories. Adolph Dial, a Lumbee scholar also said, "Our young people need to know where they come from and how we as a tribe survived the tough times." Ms. Jacobs provides a glimpse as such tough times and how things "use to be back home," especially in the 1930's.

Dr. Sandra Lucas
University of Arizona
College of Education
Tucson, Arizona

ACKNOWLEDGEMENT

I am grateful to have the opportunity to take a leave of absence from full-time teaching to pursue my dream of earning a Masters Degree at the University of Arizona in Tucson and finish my first book. I am grateful to have a mentor like Dr. Sandy Lucas, a Lumbee, who is director of Project NATIVE III, a Native Teachers Program, which I am honored to be a participant. My tribe, the Lumbees, have a long history of Lumbee educators and Lumbee mentors in Robeson County, North Carolina. It is nice to be two thousand miles away from home and know I have a Lumbee mentor who is supportive of my writing, academic and professional goals.

INTRODUCTION

I recall my studies from the Bible and how Job was tested and had one affliction after another. He had integrity, although he and suffered much. Because of the many trials he endured, he was a better man and received blessings. Likewise, my family has been faced with many trials, therefore, the title of my book is, *The Children of Job* .

This is the first of a series of books. *The Children of Job* is actually a story about the life of my father as a young boy. The main character in this book, Larry, is about a young Lumbee boy in the 1930's. Larry depicts my father.

Daddy, was a man both, stern as a preacher and had a kind heart. With no formal education he raised his family to best of his ability. This is our story, in constant motion, hopefully, with best of days yet to come. I invite you to become part of us just for a while, in this first book, as it lays the foundation for what the family eventually experiences in later books, that is, afflictions, challenges, hard times as this family truly relates to the children of Job, the children of affliction.

CHAPTER ONE

Daddy and His Mules

It was a beautiful spring morning, and the family was dressing for Sunday morning church service. A small green-eyed little boy paced nervously back and forth on the back porch. He had been carefully dressed in his Sunday clothes by his eldest sister, Grace, as he was her personal responsibility. His shirt was starched and ironed. It was green checked, his favorite color. His overalls were blue, and his little brown feet were bare. It was warm; the dogwoods had bloomed, which meant that he wouldn't have to wear shoes again until the frost came. He was as cute as he could be but could be as mean as a rattlesnake if riled. He had a kind heart that was easily hurt by any unkindness, although he tried hard not to show it.

He had been given the name of Layrue by his mother, but he preferred to be called Larry or just plain Lay. His only wish now was that it was Monday or any day except Sunday 'cause you couldn't work, and he had some unfinished work to do out in the cotton field. It had been revival week and Little Larry was just plain tired of preaching, but it wouldn't do any good to say anything to his momma. She probably would have half-killed him with a strap. He knew the only thing to do was to get ready to go and pretend like he was glad to be there. Larry knew all this, but his head sometimes proved to be as hard as the proverbial brickbat, and he planned to skip out of preaching—just this once if he could manage to slip past the all-seeing eyes of his mother. His one thought was that he had to rescue his mules and see if they could really plow.

After everyone was ready and Grandma said the morning prayers, the wagon was loaded with the family. The family mule, Ole Logan, looked pained as the last one climbed in for the two-mile ride to Reedy Branch Baptist Church. Larry was so quiet that Grandma made a mental note to check his temperature. Surely, something was wrong with the boy. As they drove off from the house, Grandpa was standing on the front porch waving. He did not attend church but made sure the family went every Sunday. Grandpa wasn't saved and didn't see much use in pretending, so he just stayed home. His job was to mind the dinner pot on the old iron stove so when the family returned, dinner would be almost ready and they wouldn't have to wait too long to eat.

"Well, I reckon that boy'll behave today," thought Grandpa. He knew Larry didn't want to go to service because he had told him in private. He explained to the child that the devil was everywhere just waiting to gobble up everyone who didn't go to church, so just to be on the safe side, Larry promised to go and do his best. Larry wondered though how Grandpa has survived so long 'cause he sure didn't go to church except for an occasional funeral, but he had sense enough not to mention this fact. Grandpa hoped that Liz wouldn't have to take a strap to the boy. He was her favorite but she seldom showed it, not wanting to spoil the child.

On the way to church, Larry was back in the cotton field, reliving the fun he had on Saturday. He had made a harness, cleared out a little patch, and was ready to try his mules just to see if they could really plow. He didn't exactly have a plow but would make one just as soon as his mules were broke to the harness. He still didn't see why Grandma wanted him to go to church since he'd been there every night except for Saturday. Friday was fun 'cause they had a big potluck dinner, but too much of anything was bad for you, or so the old people said. Larry didn't figure Grandma listened much to ole folks 'cause she sure was making him go to church—again.

Arriving on the churchyard was always fun. Everybody was glad to see everyone else, and from the way they acted, it seemed like it had been a whole week instead of just one day. John Willie, the eldest son, found a place to park the mule and went off to find his sweetie, Eula. Luke, being the second eldest, escorted the family to their section, about midway of the church. Grandma was holding Nelson, the baby, in her lap; Lefairley, the knee baby, was sitting beside her; and she put Larry on her other side. She had learned from experience that he absolutely could not sit still in church, not without getting a stern look, and sometimes it took a pinch or two. Larry was miserable but tried to pay attention out of respect for the talking-to Grandpa had given him before he left the house that morning. He loved his daddy and wanted to make him proud of him. He would endure anything to see that special look in Grandpa's eyes when he did something right.

The opening song was "Amazing Grace," and everyone began to sing. Listening to the words, Larry realized that he had never met a wretch before and wondered what they looked like. He was gonna ask when he got home so that from now on, he would be able to spot one if he ever had a chance to be in their company. He imagined though, from the words, that it was not a good thing to be called a wretch and mentally vowed that he would never become one, not if he could help it anyhow.

After the singing, the preacher got up and made announcements and passed the plate for money. Larry reached into his overall's pockets and carefully removed his penny tied tightly in his Sunday handkerchief. He untied it gently and got ready to put it into the collection plate when it came his turn. He loved paying his tithes and always remembered to pay it without being told. He had made ten cents that week, and being a whiz in math, he could figure out his tithes all by himself. He did not mind paying money to the Lord because he had always been told that God would open heaven's windows and shower blessings on him. Larry believed in blessings and needed one today to be showered down on his mules so they would be able to plow. He silently prayed that they were all right and hoped reverently that he could teach them how to plow. He didn't see anything wrong in praying for his mules 'cause they were God's creatures too.

After the collection had been gathered, it was time for Sunday school. Grace, the eldest girl, took Larry, Zonnie, Ivory, Fon, and Don to their class. Deacon Oxendine was their teacher, and he was boring as all get out. He knew his Bible but just didn't know how to pass on the stories in an exciting way. Larry dragged his feet to the back of the classroom and got ready to fall asleep if there weren't any flies buzzing around to keep him awake. The Sunday school room was hot, small, and had hard wooden benches placed in rows for you to sit on. It was hard to sleep in such conditions, but sometimes most of the class managed to do it, thanks to the deacon's dry lessons.

The Sunday school lesson this morning was about a man named Baalim who has an ass that talked to him. Larry was immediately confused because the only ass he knew about was the one that got whipped when his daddy got mad at him. And yes, it did occasionally speak, but such things were best done in the yard. His confusion was cleared up when one of the older girls asked about the ass. Deacon explained that it was like a mule, only smaller. Larry was intrigued and felt that it was a sign from God that his mules were ready to plow. He actually enjoyed the lesson and could hardly believe it when the bell rang to go to preaching. He knew that he had five minutes to go outside to the outhouse or the pump and planned to sneak away and go check on his mules. Grandma was waiting for him. "Boy, she sure knows everything," thought Larry as she led him back inside the church for service.

After the congregation sang "The Old Rugged Cross," the preacher began the service. He told about three men from the Old Testament times who had faith in God. They were told to forget about him or die, but they refused and chose to be thrown in a fiery furnace. The preacher said they were not burned a bit, and after the king took them out, he believed in God too. Larry paid attention because he knew when he got home, Grandpa would ask him about the sermon. He had a sudden thought that maybe the devil had been held off from getting his daddy for as long as he got his preaching secondhand from Larry and others every Sunday.

Finally the service was over, and the family began to gather their things together for the ride home. Grandma has nursed Nelson, and he was fast asleep. Little Lefairley, or Lee as he was called, was nodding. Larry almost ran outside to find his spot in the wagon. Ole Logan had his feed bag on and would need some water before they started. Being in a hurry, Larry grabbed Logan's bucket and ran to the pump. Now if you have ever pumped water, you can appreciate the fact that the church has a pump that was very easy to work. It gave out a lot of water at one time, not like the one at home. Grandma said that the family's pump was "stingy," which meant that you only got a small amount of water, and it took a lot more effort. Larry quickly filled the bucket and carefully carried it to Logan. By the time Grandma had said her goodbyes and arrived at the wagon, everyone was ready to go. Eula was going home with the family to spend the afternoon with John Willie, and he was grinning from ear to ear.

"Ms. Liz," said Eula, "it was so nice of you to invite me for dinner."

"Why, honey, we always love to have you over," Grandma answered. "It wouldn't be Sunday without you." Eula looked pleased with the compliment, and from the way he looked, you could have sold John Willie for a penny and got change back. The ride back seemed to last forever to Larry. He hardly paid any attention to the conversations being carried on. His mind was on his mules. He knew that he would have some time before dinner to check on them. He just wouldn't tell anyone where he was going. Sunday was a free day, just so long as you didn't do any work, and he wasn't going to. The mules were, but since they weren't Christians, it wouldn't matter, he figured.

Grandpa was standing on the front porch when they arrived home. Larry jumped out of the wagon and ran up the five steps.

"Whoa, boy," Grandpa said. "What's your hurry today? Did your momma have to whip you again?" "No, sir," Larry answered. "I just wanted to tell you about what I learned at church before I forgot it, Daddy."

"All right, son, let's hear it."

"Well, Daddy, in Sunday school, I learned that there is an animal called an ass. It's something like a mule, only littler, and it talked to a man and saved his life," Larry responded.

"Yes, son, that's right. Did you know what a real ass was or did somebody have to tell you. I use the word sometimes in the wrong way when I'm mad," said Grandpa shamefully.

"Somebody told me, Daddy, but that's okay 'cause I use it myself the same way." Larry realized what he had said and clapped his little hands over his mouth. Grandpa was trying so hard not to laugh that tears welled up in his eyes.

"That's all right, son. We'll both try to do better. Now tell me what the preacher had to say."

"Daddy, the preacher said that Shadrach and his two brothers, Mendigo and Meshack, I believe that's how you say their names, loved God so much they went into a fire to die for him and God saved them," Larry proudly answered and then added, "Someday I will go into a fire myself for him." Grandpa was touched, and now the tears rolled down his brown cheeks. He held his son close to his heart for a second and rubbed his curly head. He also looked into those green eyes and thought to himself, "What a beautiful sight." Those eyes were so filled with innocence that Grandpa felt that he was actually inside a church for a moment.

"Well, boy, you've got about a half hour 'til dinnertime if you want to go stretch your legs. Just you remember to be close enough by to hear me call you," Grandpa said gruffly, still filled with emotion.

"All right! I will," Larry yelped as he began to run down the steps.

At last, he was on his way to check on his mules. Larry ran down the dirt road, past the garden and cornfield. His little feet made small circlets of dust rise from the dry soil. It seemed to take him forever to reach the twelve-acre field of cotton. All the way there, his heart was pounding with anticipation. He was also worried about his mules. He had found a safe place for them to stay until he got back, but he was scared that they had got out or, if not, that they had got too hot.

He was there at last. There was the place where he put the mules the day before. Now actually, they weren't real mules but frogs Larry had caught at the pond, but they didn't know that. If he said they were mules with enough faith, then mules they were. All he wanted to do right now was fit the little string harness to them and see if they would hop in a straight line. Larry reached his little cleared patch between the two fields of cotton. Yes, the mound was still there undisturbed. He had buried the frogs in a deep hole just to keep them safe. As he began to dig them up, he began to fear that they just might be dead. He recalled a sermon that the preacher had given once. He told about the ten laws that everyone had to live by. One of them said plain as day, "Thou shall not kill nothing," unless you wanted to go to the bad place. He felt terrible owing to the feelings, reawakened by the church service today. He didn't know what God would think of him if his mules were dead, and he didn't want to think about it. He stopped digging and said a heartfelt prayer, this time for the safety of his mules.

After his prayer, he felt better and continued with his digging. He felt that he should be getting close to the mules when all at once, one hopped out of the hole straight at him. The rest followed quickly and seemed to make for poor Larry. His mules were chasing him because they were mad that he had buried them for so long. Larry was terrified and began to run down the dirt road toward home. He stumbled and fell and quickly scrambled up and ran for all he was worth. He looked back, and those mules were still coming. He cut across the cotton field, jumping over the small plants. His heart seemed to be in his throat, and he knew for sure that they would catch him and eat him up. He didn't look back anymore but ran as hard as he could. As he neared the house, he slowed down so that he would not have to do any explaining, which would surely get him into trouble.

Larry ran around to the backyard, to the pump, which was located just a few feet from the house. He stuck his head under the spout and pumped water with all of his might. He washed his face and dried both face and head with a clean piece of flour sack left there for that purpose. He quietly walked to the back steps and climbed up the eight steps onto the back porch. Thank the Lord, nobody was outside! He sat down on the porch swing and began to gently sway. It didn't occur to the child to give thanks for the safety of the frogs. Larry was just glad to be safe at home. He could smell the fried chicken, his favorite meal, and knew that the comforting presence of his momma and daddy were just inside. He felt a sense of security, and with each squeak of the swing, his eyes began to droop. He knew that Grandpa would call him when dinner was ready. Larry fell asleep. It would be years before anyone knew about his mules or why he was deathly afraid of frogs for the remainder of his life.

Chapter Two

Whipping Ole Logan

Springtime on the farm was truly a sight to behold. With each passing day, a new miracle occurred. Old Betsy, the family dog, gave birth to a litter of seven puppies. Souie, Porkie, and Millie, the sows, all had litters of ten piglets each. Larry was so excited by everything around him. He wanted to help in the fields with the plowing, but he was too little. Grandpa promised that next year he would teach him how to plow, and he could hardly wait. The older boys all could handle Ole Logan, and Larry wanted to give him a try all by himself. Don, his older brother, decided to help Larry achieve his dream. Now, his brother, Don, had picked up the bad habit of chewing tobacco because he thought that it made him older. He knew how much Larry wanted to plow with Ole Logan and decided to help him get his chance.

"Hey, boy," yelled Don, Do you want to learn how to handle Ole Logan with the plow?"

I reckon. "If I'm big enough," Larry answered.

"Well, let me tell you how you go about doing it," Don replied.

Now you just have to understand how Don was. He was a big, gangly fellow with a sense of humor. He also had one of the kindest hearts in the whole world. Don loved his little brother and really wanted to help him grow up, but I guess he just went about it sort of backwards. He convinced Larry that if he would chew some tobacco, swallow the juice, followed by the wad of tobacco, surely he would be able to handle Ole Logan just like John Willie and Luke. Larry decided that it was worth a try.

"Well, boy, do you want to try it or not?" Don asked.

"I guess so," Larry replied. "I'm tired of always having to wait until I'm bigger to do what I want to do. Hand me that tobacco, and you just tell me how much to bite off," said Larry with a confidence he didn't really feel.

"Well, boy, you just bite off as much as your mouth can hold," replied Don.

Larry grabbed the plug of Black Mariah and bit off a big wad and began to chew as hard as he could. As he began this process, his green eyes began to water. "That's right, you just keep on chewing," encouraged Don. "Now remember you gotta swallow the juice and then the tobacco. After you do that, you can whip Ole Logan if you want to," said Don. Larry continued to chew and swallow. After a couple of minutes, things began to look sort of fuzzy. His eyes were running water freely now, and he was beginning to feel sick. "Boy, you better keep on swallowing," said Don.

"I don't feel so good, Don. You sure you know what you talking about?"

"I sure do. Don't you see me plowing in the fields with Logan? How do you think I can do it so easy? Don't I always chew tobacco?" asked Don.

"I'll take your word for it, Don. If you say it's so, then I guess it is." Larry continued to swallow the juice, becoming sicker by the minute. He finally swallowed the wad of tobacco, and everything went black.

As Don watched his little brother fall to the ground, his heart almost stopped beating. He knew that something bad had happened. He couldn't understand it. He had never gotten sick from tobacco, but then he had never swallowed a wad before. He knew that if something happened to Larry and it was his fault, his mother would beat him within an inch of his life. He reached down and carefully picked Larry up in his arms. He began to cry as he walked to the house. They had been down by the chicken coop when the caper began, only a short distance from the house. Luckily, it was between dinnertime and suppertime, and everyone was outside, away from the house, except Grace, who was inside preparing dinner. Don carried Larry to the back porch swing and laid him gently down. He then ran to the pump to get a fresh bucket of cold water. Returning in record time, he gently bathed his brother's face, all the while talking to him about how sorry he was. Larry began to regain consciousness and to vomit. Don held the bucket under his head and patted him on the back. After a few minutes, Larry felt better, but he was still sick. Don sat holding him in his arms in the porch swing for over an hour. Larry promised not to tell anyone what had happened because he knew his brother would have never hurt him on purpose.

—

Grandma was the first to return home. She had been to the Hunt's helping Mrs. Hunt bring her first grandchild into the world. She saw Don and Larry on the swing and, with the intuition of a mother, knew immediately that something was wrong with her son. Her child's face was green!

"Don, what happened to him?" she asked quickly.

"I don't know, Momma. I found him lying by the coop and brought him here," he answered, which was not the entire truth; in fact it wasn't even close enough to be confused with it.

"Son, what's the matter with you?" she questioned with her heart in her eyes.

"Momma, I reckon I ate something that made me sick, that's all." Larry replied out of both loyalty and love for his brother. Grandma picked him up and gently held him, felt his head, and determined that it was a stomachache. She went inside and made him a soda pop, which was a mixture of water, vinegar, sugar, and baking soda, and gave it to Larry who drank it down gratefully.

"I'll stay with him, Momma, while he drinks his soda pop," said Don. "I know it's time for you to get supper ready to put on the table."

"Thank you, son," Grandma replied. She gently touched Larry's head and turned to go inside.

"Son," she said, "do you think you will be all right?"

"Yes, ma'am. Don will take good care of me, Momma." Grandma went inside to help Grace get supper ready to put on the table for the family.

Don whispered that he appreciated Larry not telling on him. He sat and held him on his lap and gently rocked him back and forth on the swing. There was a gentle breeze blowing, the birds were singing, and Larry felt that maybe one more year would not be too long to wait for his chance to learn how to plow.

Suppertime came, and Grandpa and the older boys came in from the fields. Grandpa came to check on Larry just to see if he was okay. As he turned to go inside, he looked at Don gravely and said, "Son, please don't give that boy any more tobacco. He's too young, and it's going to make him sick every time."

"I'm sorry, Daddy. How in the world did you know?"

"Well, as hard as it is to believe, I was a boy one time myself. We will keep this under our caps, all right, son?"

"Yes, sir, Daddy, and thank you," Don replied.

"Let's go on in and eat our supper. Your mother worked hard to get it on the table." Larry had woken up by now and was feeling a lot better. The three went inside as the evening softly fell.

—

CHAPTER THREE

Picking Cucumbers

One morning, soon after the incident with the tobacco, Larry woke up to his mother's voice calling. He wondered why he was getting up when it was still dark outside. He quickly pulled on his pants, as he had slept in his shirt and underwear, and walked into the kitchen to find out what was going on. Grandma was at the stove finishing up breakfast. "Momma, what in the world is going on?" Larry asked.

"Don't you remember what today is, boy?" Grandma answered.

"No, ma'am, I surely don't," Larry responded.

"Today is the first day of cucumber season. We decided that this year you are old enough to help with the picking. I've got you a special bucket, just your size, that you can pick in," Grandma replied.

"Oh boy!" yelled Larry as he raced away to tell Don that he was a big boy now. Grandma just smiled and shook her head as she thought of the hard work of picking cucumbers. She hoped her son would still be excited this afternoon when the picking had been done. Grandpa walked into the room.

"Alex, you got them nickels that I've been saving all year?" questioned Grandma with a look of expectation in her eyes.

"Yes, Liz, I do. We'll put them out just like we talked about. I'll go now and hide them on every row so when the young 'uns pick, they will find money. That will make the job seem more like fun."

Alex and Liz looked into each other's eyes. The words "I love you" were seldom used by the couple, but that look into the souls of each other said more than words can ever say. "I'll be back in a few minutes," Alex said.

"Breakfast will be on the table when you get here," replied Liz.

The family gathered round the kitchen table for breakfast. The kitchen was the room in which the family was often together. It was very large, with two windows, one facing the east with the other centered on the west. The table was rectangular and covered with a red gingham tablecloth. Two wooden benches were placed at each side, each long enough to fit six growing children comfortably, two chairs stood at each end, one for Grandpa and the other for Grandma. Around the front part of the kitchen, cabinets lined the floor. Inside were jars and jars of food stored the previous year by Grandma and covered on the outside by the same red gingham to match the table. The curtains were white with red gingham ties to keep them open in the daytime. On the windowsill stood jars of pickles and chowchow, canned last summer by Grace and Ivory. Off to the east side stood the wood-burning stove used for both the preparation of food and warmth during the cold of the late fall and winter. In the western corner hung Grandma's prized possession, a round gold-edged mirror, used and appreciated most by the older members of the family. Beneath the mirror stood a small table used to hold Grandpa's soap cup and razor. One of Grandma's secret delights was to watch him shave every Wednesday night and Sunday morning, but of course, she had never mentioned that to him.

Grandpa came in just as the family was sitting down. He took his place at the head of the table. Grandma was just placing the flaky buttermilk biscuits down as he walked in. She looked at Larry and said, "Son, since you're old enough to work in the fields, maybe you can you say the blessing this morning?" Larry was shocked. He had never been asked that before and wasn't sure what to say.

"Yes, ma'am, I'll do my best," he replied. "Dear Lord, we thank thee for this food and ask thee to bless it. In thy name we pray, Amen"—he paused for a while—"and dear Lord, please help me find a bunch of cucumbers today. Amen again." Larry said proudly, "How was that, Momma?"

"Son, it was a fine blessing, thank you. I'm sure that the good Lord will help you do your best today."

Breakfast was delicious. Grandma had made grits, bacon, pancakes, and sausage, and there was plenty of fresh milk from Jezebel, the family cow. Larry was so excited about picking cucumbers today that the meal seemed never to end. The more enlightened members of the family wished that it had never come because they knew what that cucumber field was all about. Breakfast ended, and Grace began to clean up. Being the eldest girl, it was her job to stay home and prepare the noonday meal. But she didn't have a problem with that since she didn't love picking cucumbers.

Everyone else gathered on the back porch, and each picked up their bucket. Grandma had found a little blue speckled water bucket for Larry, and his eyes lit up when she handed it to him. "Son, this won't get heavy when you fill it up. I hope you like it."

"I do, Momma, and I'm gonna fill up a lot for you." The family filed down the back steps and headed for the cucumber field, only a short distance from the house. It was still dark, but you could see a rim of red at the eastern horizon. The moon was still visible, and some stars could still be seen up at the center and darkest part of the sky. There was a quiet coolness, and everything seemed to still be safe in the arms of deep sleep. The dirt path to the cucumber field was covered with a light, powdery dust, which felt good to bare feet. Only an occasional twitter from the birds could be heard. As Larry walked along the well-worn dirt path, his eyes were constantly roaming all around, taking note of the wonder that his small heart could appreciate though his mind was not mature enough to identify the source of his awe and feelings of reverence.

As they neared the field, Larry began to run. He wanted to get ahead of everybody else and get the first row. He had heard his sisters and brothers talking about how "gappy" the first row was. The way they said *gappy*, Larry figured that it must be a good thing, and Larry wanted to get there first.

"Slow down, boy, them cucumbers ain't going nowhere," Alex called.

"I just want the gappy row, Daddy, 'cause I believe that's the best one," Larry replied. Grandpa and Grandma busted out laughing and looked at their other children with that knowing look in their eyes.

As they reached the cucumber patch, the sun was beginning to emerge in a blaze of red, signaling the approach of dawn. Larry reached the first row and set his bucket down at the first plant. He noticed that Grandma picked the row right beside him. It was his first day, and she meant to be as close to him as possible. The rest of the family arrived at the field, selected their rows, and began picking. Now if you have never picked cucumbers, let me explain the process. The rows are planted with thick cucumber bushes. You have to divide the leaves, turning them over to find the cucumbers beneath. It probably should be called searching for cucumbers, but we won't change the name. It's real easy to miss some, which explains why Grandma chose to put Little Larry by her side.

Larry began to pick, watching his mother, and was having a good time. As each cucumber hit the bottom of his small pail, he felt a sense of elation. "Boy!" he thought, "I bet I'll outpick them all today specially since Momma is right beside me." As he began to move up his row, Grandma was searching the middle of the row since a lot of cucumbers grew there.

"Larry, come back here, son. I want to show you something."

"Okay, Momma." Larry moved back down the row beside Grandma who stood with the runner of a plant overturned.

"Look here, son. Do you see these cucumbers?"

"Yes, ma'am, I do. They are real little, Momma."

"I know, son, but these are called number ones, and when you sell the cucumbers, they bring the most money. I reckon the pickle company likes them because they are real crunchy and make the best pickles."

"Momma, don't you make our pickles?" asked Larry.

"Yes, son, I do, but a lot of city folks buy their pickles at the store. That's why we are able to pick and sell these cucumbers and make money for y'alls school clothes," Grandma answered. "So pick as hard as you can and fill up your bucket. Be ready to empty when I am, okay?"

"Yes, ma'am, Momma, I will." Larry bent over and began to pick cucumbers. "Momma, can I ask you one more thing?" asked Larry as he stood up. "Why did the other young 'uns want this row 'cause it's gappy?"

Grandma just stood up and laughed out loud as she looked lovingly at her son. "Boy, just look down that row. See how the plants have spaces between them? The first row always has fewer plants on it 'cause the planter hasn't been used all winter. The seeds don't drop out like they're supposed to, so you have fewer plants to pick. You'll get to the end of the row faster, and it'll seem like you are picking faster than anyone else. You know, your daddy always has a prize for the one that finishes first. That's why everybody wanted that row."

"What's the prize, Momma, for this year?" asked Larry.

"I don't know, but I reckon it's something special 'cause your daddy always likes to surprise you. He didn't even tell me what the prize is for this year," responded Grandma with a twinkle in her eye. She had an idea but was not sure what the surprise was, but knowing Alex, it would be a good one, it always was.

Grandma and Larry both bent down over their rows and began to pick. Larry found out, from the brief lesson provided by Grandma, that he could find a lot more cucumbers. He thought about the prize and wondered what it could be. He wanted a fishing pole; all the older boys had one, and he was tired of making his fishing pole from the reeds that grew beside the river. He loved to fish and longed to have his own pole that wouldn't break when he caught a big fish. Larry wanted to be just like his older brothers and fish with a store-bought fishing pole. He wondered if the prize was some money so that he could buy a pole.

He began to pick with all of his boundless energy, which was how he tackled any job. Grandma just watched him for a while to make sure he was doing it right. Satisfied, she bent down to pick her row. Larry began to wonder if he would ever reach the end of the cucumber row. It seemed to go on forever. He stooped down and turned over a vine, and to his complete surprise, he found a shiny new nickel. He could hardly believe his luck. "Momma, you'll never guess what I found," Larry yelled excitedly.

"What in the world is it, son?" Grandma asked.

"Momma, I just found a nickel. Do you reckon it belongs to anybody 'cause I would sure hate to give it back, but I will if I have to."

"No, son, that is a surprise from me and your daddy to make picking easier and kinda fun for y'all. We put one on each row for y'all to find."

At that moment, Don yelled out, "Hey! Look what I found." He held up a shiny nickel grinning for all he was worth. "Boy, I never expected to find money just picking cucumbers. I figured that the market was the only place that I'd be paid for picking." Alex and Lizzie looked at each other and smiled. They were sure that the first day of picking would be a success.

The family picked about half the field, and it was time for dinner. Grace had stayed back to cook the meal and had it ready when everyone came in. Everyone emptied their buckets for the last time before lunch. The sacks were lined up at the end of the rows, so far there were twelve. Grandpa thought that the first picking would be the best one—there were a lot of number ones, and he knew that they would bring the best price. The family started the short hot journey back to the house for dinner and an hour's rest. Little Larry was tired, but he would never admit it to anyone. He had enjoyed picking beside Grandma and felt that he had done a good job. He had also found two nickels, and he was planning on buying that fishing pole at the end of picking season. It had been a good morning.

Larry began to think about dinner and received a sudden burst of energy. He ran to the pump, and thankfully, Grace had found time in her busy morning to pump a foot tub of water that had been warmed by the sun. Lying beside the tub was a fresh bar of lye soap and several pieces of flour sack designed with blue for-get-me-nots. Larry grabbed the soap and began to dash water on his face with his small grubby hands, stained by the cucumbers. He suddenly realized that his hands just wouldn't get clean.

"Momma! I can't git my hands clean. You know, Daddy won't let me to the table if I'm not good and clean."

"Wait a minute, son, and I'll show you how to get the cucumber stains off your hands." Grandma reached beside the foot tub and opened a small jar of washing powder. She sprinkled a small amount on Larry's hands and told him to gently rub them together. Larry was amazed at the stains. They were beginning to wash off.

"Now, son, take this lye soap and rub some more on your hands and rinse them off in the tub." Larry rubbed the soap on his hands and put them into the foot tub. To his complete surprise, his hands were clean, except for his fingernails, and Grandpa wouldn't say nothing about them.

"Thanks, Momma, I'm gonna run inside and see what Grace cooked."

Grandma looked at her boy and just smiled. The rest of the family cleaned up and went inside to eat their noonday meal and rest for a while before returning to the field. Grace had fried squash, boiled cabbage with neck bones, chicken giblets with rice, and cornbread. She has also made two gallons of iced tea, and for a special treat, they had cinnamon water with sugar for Larry and the smaller boys 'cause Grandma had said they were too young for tea. Don asked the blessing on the food, and everyone began to eat. After dinner, everyone had an hour to rest. Larry went outside and went to the huge oak tree that had a small tree house, built by John Willie and Luke, his older brothers. Larry climbed up, went inside, and lay on a small checked quilt. Pretty soon, he was fast asleep, dreaming of his new fishing pole.

All too soon, Larry heard Grandma calling him. He woke up and raced down the ladder. It was time to return to the field. Everyone had time to rest, but the afternoon sun was hot. Everyone, except for Larry of course, knew how hard the work would be this afternoon. Larry skipped along dreaming of his store-bought fishing pole. The rows seemed twice as long as they had been that morning. Larry thought that he would never fill up his bucket. The afternoon sun was scorching, and he was sweating like a pig. Grandma was picking steadily beside him, but something was missing from the fun that he'd had earlier. Larry was just plain tired and didn't know what to do to pick any harder than he was doing. He had wanted to keep up with Grandma, but it was getting harder by the minute. The sun beat down on him. Grandpa said it was a monkey on your back, and now Larry well understood the saying. Finally, they were on the last rows. The end was in sight, and everyone was glad to see it. Lined up in the middle and end of the field, the gunnysacks filled with cucumbers proudly stood. Grandpa looked and mentally calculated what they would bring at the market.

"Liz, I believe this year will be a good one if the corn, tobacco, and cotton bear like these cucumbers have."

"Alex, we'll do all right this year. I have prayed all winter for a good year and feel that today is proof that the good Lord has answered my prayers." Alex looked at his wife and mentally thanked God for bringing them together. He knew that without her, he was nothing, for her faith always brought them through the hard times that farm people often had to endure. He also wished that one day, he would have half the faith in God that she had.

As the family reached the ends of the cucumber rows, Grandpa, Luke, and John Willie were beginning to bring the full cucumber sacks to the end of the field. Later, they would load them on the wagon and take them to the cucumber market to sell. Mr. Britt, the landlord, would meet them there to make sure that they got a fair price. Cucumbers were a crop that you did not have to split the profits with the landowner. The government paid the property owners a fee for the land to grow them on. This method helped the poor farmers make a decent living. All other crops were sold on halves. Grandpa was a tenant farmer. Mr. Britt, a very nice and generous man, paid for the tools, seed, fertilizer, and other things needed to bring in a crop. When harvest came, he received half of the money that the crop brought. It was a system that was only as fair as the landlord, as many of the Lumbee Indians at that time could not read or write due to having to leave school early in order to help earn the family living. The Jacobs family was blessed to have an honest one. Grandpa couldn't read; Grandma could, but women weren't allowed to conduct business. It was a hard life, but families stuck together and did whatever was necessary.

Larry was so excited. This was to be his first trip to the cucumber shed. Grandma had said he could go if he picked good, and he had. Luke hitched Ole Logan to the wagon and went to the end of the cucumber field to load the sacks. It was getting close to dark, but that didn't matter, the shed stayed open until late. Grandpa was letting John Willie go and sell the cucumbers.

"Son, I reckon you're a man now, and it's time for you to start learning how to handle business. You'll have a family one day and need to know these things. Now, the important thing to remember is to be right beside the man as he unloads the sacks. See how they divide and make sure that you watch every move. Some of them will cheat you if they get the chance. You be right beside Mr. Britt. He'll be sure nobody cheats us out of any money."

"I will, Daddy. You can count on that," replied John Willie.

Grandpa nodded and went to the pump to wash up for supper, confident in his son's ability to handle this important matter.

Luke drove the wagon to the market, with John Willie seated beside him; behind rode Alfonzo, normally called Fon, with Zonnie, Don, and Larry sitting in the back resting among the filled sacks, which showed their first day's labor. The boys were happy and sang on the way there. It was an hour before sunset, and the day had cooled down considerably. All were excited and speculated on how much money they would make. John Willie was a little nervous but proud that Grandpa had trusted him with this great responsibility. He was almost old enough to marry and start his own family and wanted to learn as much as he could about business. John has a good head for math and was excellent at building things. He often dreamed of the house that he would build for Eula, that is, if she would have him. He was scared to death to ask her to marry him but knew that he would soon have to get it over with.

As these thoughts were tumbling through his head, they arrived at the cucumber shed. There were three wagons ahead of them, but they didn't mind; that would give them a chance to get out and visit with the neighbors and talk about the first day of picking. Larry jumped out of the wagon and ran to find his friend, Luther Chavis. The two boys ran off together to try and see everything that was going on. It was Luther's first trip to the shed as well as his first day of picking cucumbers. They had a lot to talk about. Luther could hardly believe it when Larry told him about finding the nickels on his cucumber rows.

"Boy! I wish my momma had thought of doing that," he exclaimed. "That would have made picking them cucumbers a whole lot more fun."

Larry just laughed and said, "I got the best momma in the whole world. She always knows how to make everything more fun, don't she?"

"Yes, and I'm gonna tell my momma as soon as I get home tonight. Maybe the next time we pick, she'll leave something for us to find. Won't that be something?"

"All right, you young 'uns, y'all better git over there and see how them cucumbers get divided 'cause that's how you know how much money you're likely to make," yelled Ozmer Lowery.

"Yes, sir," the boys echoed and ran over to the shed just as the next wagon was beginning to unload. The Carter boys were just beginning to lift the heavy cucumber sacks and pour them into the hopper that would send them down a conveyer belt and sort them by size. By the look of things, it was a good picking. Their daddy, Grady, stood by and watched carefully as the bags were emptied. Mr. Carter was a preacher in the little community of Saddletree.

He was well respected and was one of the few who could read and write, although the shed was run by an honest man, Elmer Hammonds, who would never cheat anyone. When the wagon was empty, the Carter boys drove it away from the side of the shed. Larry was excited because now it was their turn to empty the cucumbers and see how much money they would have to take home to Grandpa. Don and Luke each grabbed a sack and began to pour the cucumbers in. Larry watched every move they made. He marveled at their strength and wanted to be big enough to lift and pour a heavy sack of cucumbers, and he knew that one day soon, his time would come. He watched as the cukes were sorted and saw that they had a whole lot of number ones, which Grandma had told him would bring the most money. He could see that new fishing pole already. "Boy, I'll have that pole in my hands real soon. Them fish better watch out 'cause I'm sure gonna catch them all," he thought to himself with a big grin on his face.

Finally the wagon was unloaded, and John Willie and Mr. Britt were both talking to the man who owned the shed, Mr. Pate. It was ran by Hammonds, an Indian, business was conducted by the owner when it came to making out the checks. Mr. Pate wanted to be sure that his fee was paid, and each person receive the rest of the money that was owed him. As John Willie looked at the check in his hand, his eyes shone with joy. He shook hands with Mr. Britt and thanked him for being there.

"John, you tell your daddy that today's picking is one of the best that I've ever seen in all my years of farming. Your family works hard, and I appreciate it. I know that you'll be careful with that check and hand it to Alex when you get home."

"Yes, sir, I will," replied John. "My daddy trusted me, and I won't let him down." John placed the folded check in the front pocket of his overalls and went to find the boys for the trip home. It had been a good day, and for the first time, he really felt like a man. Whistling, he called to Luke for him get the wagon ready to go home.

"Boys y'all better git in. It's time to go home and eat supper. Y'all 'member that tonight, Daddy's gonna give out the prize to the best picker today, okay?"

The boys rode quietly home, tired and satisfied with the labors of the day. Each wondered to whom the prize would go to this year. John already knew as Grandpa had taken him into his confidence. He was pleased and agreed with the decision and knew that the family would be too. He could hardly wait to get home. Larry fell asleep as the wagon slowly made its way through the darkness. Soon the light from the kitchen window could be seen by the boys. They knew that supper was ready and waiting on the stove for them. Luke pulled up beside the barn, and the boys got out. John would help unhitch Ole Logan and make sure that he was rubbed down, fed, and watered. As the boys walked to the pump to wash up, Granddaddy was standing on the back porch.

"Well, boys, y'all worked hard today, and I'm proud of you all. Your momma and I decided that this year, the prize would go to Larry. He never complained and had his bucket ready to empty every time Liz did. That takes some doing."

Larry could hardly believe his ears. He had won and didn't care what the prize was. Just then, Grandma walked out on the porch with a brand-new fishing pole in her hands. It was the one from the store and in his favorite color, green. Larry's eyes filled with tears, and he ran to his mother and hugged her tightly. He then grabbed Grandpa's hand and shook it for all he was worth.

"Thank you, Momma and Daddy. I'll keep this pole for the rest of my life and catch all the fish you can eat, see if I don't."

"Son, you worked like a man on your first day and made us proud. That's enough for us," said Grandpa. Grandma nodded, wiping away a tear of joy, and told them to come inside for supper. It had been a wonderful and a very prosperous day.

—

CHAPTER FOUR

Making Pickles and Canning

A few weeks later, the garden was coming off, and it was time to begin to prepare food for the winter. Grandma and the girls got out the big washpots and filled them with water. The boys had brought some wood to start a fire with and boil the pots clean. Early on Monday morning, shortly before sunrise, Grandma, Grace, and Ivory went to the garden to pick the sweet peas, pull corn, and gather the other vegetables that were ready. The boys were going to finish picking the cucumbers as it was the last week. The early-morning dew lay heavily on the lush vegetable leaves, and the produce was easily visible. There had been plenty of rain, and the garden was in full production.

First, they picked the sweet peas, Grandpa's favorite, and placed them in small tubs under the shade of the large oak tree between the house and the garden. The corn was pulled next and placed into large sacks. The garden peas weren't quite ready; therefore, it took only a short time to pick them.

"Well, girls, I reckon that we'll have them peas for supper this evening. There ain't enough to mess with canning right now," said Grandma.

"I'm glad, Momma. I sure am ready for some fresh peas," responded Ivory.

"Can I go and see if any tomatoes are ripe?"

"Sure, honey, go on ahead while me and Grace take the sweet peas to the back porch to shell. The boys can bring the corn over when they stop for dinner." They picked up two baskets each and walked slowly to the porch.

"Grace, you run on inside and check on the beans on the stove. Also, while you're in there, put the cornbread inside the oven. You'll have to add a little wood you know."

"All right, Momma, it's almost time for dinner, and you know how Daddy likes to have it on the table when he gets here," laughed Grace.

After dinner, it was time to shell the peas and shuck the corn. Anna Liza, her cousin, had come to help Grandma and the girls with the work. She was especially good at cutting the corn off the cob, which would make the work go more quickly. Everything had to be in the jars and sealed before dark and placed on the dinner table to cool off. The jars had been boiled and were clean, sanitary, and lined up on the worktable that Grandpa had built for Grandma this past Christmas. It was her pride and joy to have such a large fine table to do her canning on. This winter, she would also use it when they killed hogs. Grandma had been able to buy new seals this year, but the old bands that had been taken off and carefully saved from the jars that had been emptied of their food were just fine. You only needed to use the bands long enough for lids to seal properly, and then you could remove them. Grandma still had most of the bands that she began married life with; some had rusted, but that would be all right as they would still serve their purpose of allowing the lids to seal. As soon as the lids sealed, she would just remove her bands and pack them up for next year. Living on a farm, you had to know how to make things last. Nothing was ever wasted.

Grandma began to shell the sweet peas while Grace and Ivory began to clean the ears of corn, most of which was loaded with plumb white kernels. It was Dixielee sweet corn, the kind the whole family liked. Later they would can regular field corn because Grandpa liked it too. Grandma had her big dishpan to shell peas in. She had washed them carefully, several times to remove the bugs and dirt. She was real particular about her food. It had to be perfect. After filling her pan with peas, she began to shell them. She has her own technique, which was to begin at the bottom and use her thumb to open the pod and pop the peas out. She could shell faster than anyone in the neighborhood and was often asked to help out when she had the time. Back then, neighbors were really neighbors and knew how to lend a hand when they were needed. As she began to shell, the girls knew she was about to tell them a story about how things used to be. They could hardly wait for Grandma to begin, for she knew how to tell a good story and make work seem like fun.

About sunset, the boys and Grandpa came home from picking. The older boys were to take the last cucumber crop to the shed. Grandpa went inside and, with the help of Larry, finished the preparations for supper. Grandma had put a pot of beef stew on the stove. Grandpa finished the rice and vegetables without a complaint. Little Larry was puzzled; he didn't think that men did women's work.

"Daddy, why are you cooking?" he asked.

"Son, your momma is working hard to put up food for the winter. She needs my help, and I'm glad to give it. When you're old enough to have a wife, you will understand that you have to work together, and there is no such things as 'women's work.' I don't know where you heard that anyway," answered Grandpa.

"I heard old Mr. Jones say that anything to do in a house was 'women's work.'"

"Well, son, it's not. A family works together and does everything that is needed to keep the family going. Don't you see your momma working in the fields as hard as I do?" said Grandpa.

"Yes, sir, she surely does. Momma can outwork anybody," responded Larry.

"Yes, son, and I have never heard her complain either," said Grandpa. "I'm a lucky man to have her. We have never done without and never will, as long as your momma is living and don't you ever call cooking or anything else 'women's work,' you hear?"

"I'm sorry, Daddy. Can I learn how to cook?" Larry replied.

"Just you watch your momma, boy, and you'll be the best cook around," said Grandpa. It would be many years before Larry married, but he would never forget the lesson that he learned that day.

Before long, Grandma and the girls came inside. They looked so tired, but the canning for that day was in the jars safely sealed. Grandpa sent Larry outside to make sure the fire under the washpots was out. "Liz, you sit down a minute. I'll have supper ready for you in about fifteen minutes."

"Thank you, Alex. I sure do appreciate it." Grandma sat down in her rocker that was always placed by the eastern window and silently thanked God for her husband's love. It was seldom that he needed to help out, but when necessary, he never complained. She realized how fortunate she was to have a man who had been properly raised by a caring mother. Most women that she knew had never had the pleasure of having a meal prepared for them by their husbands. Truth is, most Indian men in Robeson County would have rather died than be caught at a stove. As she sat contemplating her blessings, the rest of the family came in for supper. The meal was good, and everybody was tired but filled with a sense of contentment and pride that only comes with successfully completing a hard day's work.

The next morning's job was to plow the cotton. As John Willie was the eldest, he got to supervise the plowing. Luke hitched up Ole Logan to the plow and led him to the cotton field to begin the day's plowing. Larry was allowed to go along to watch. Grandpa warned him not to get in the way, and he promised that he wouldn't, but of course that was hard to do owing to his fascination with plowing, but let's not mention the mules again. Larry did sit by the side of the field and watched. It was also his job to get the boys fresh water every couple of hours. Grandma would make it special using a small amount of peppermint flavor and brown sugar. It was a small thing, but the boys always felt special and more refreshed and little more loved than if they had received just cold well water. Larry ran to the field with the jug of water and gave it first to John Willie because he was the eldest. The other boys all took a turn and seemed to enjoy the water and short break immensely.

John loved his little brother and knew that soon they would be separated following his marriage to Eula, that is, of course if he ever worked up enough courage to ask her. He wanted to do something special for him, so he had planned to let Larry ride on Ole Logan's back for the remainder of the morning. Larry was so excited he could hardly stand still for Luke to lift him up on the mule's back. As they began to move down the field, Larry just knew that he had died and gone to heaven. Nothing from this moment on could top this. "Well," he thought to himself. "I could die right now and be happy." The rest of the morning went smoothly, and soon it was time to go home for dinner. It has been a wonderful morning.

A week later, on Sunday afternoon, Grandma announced that it was time to make pickles for the family. The cucumbers would be gone soon, and the vegetables from the garden that were ready had been canned. Making pickles took a couple of days, so Monday would be a good time to begin. Grandpa was sure that it would not rain. He and the boys would pick the cucumbers while Grandma and the girls got jars, spices, and lime ready to prepare the pickles.

Before the sun came up on Monday morning, breakfast was on the table. Grandpa and the boys ate quickly and went out to the field to pick the small cukes that made the best pickles. Grandma and the girls went outside to prepare things that were needed. Grace pumped two tin tubs of water, while Ivory went to the small shed to get the jars. Grandma had made a fire under the washpot that was half-full of water. The jars were carefully set inside turned upside down to allow the water to thoroughly clean and sanitize them. The water came to a boil, and the jars were allowed to boil for about thirty minutes. After that, Grandma pulled what wood was left burning, away from the pot to allow the pot to cool down. Grace has a wooden crate filled with clean clothes to wrap the jars in as they would be needed when the pickles were prepared, at which time the pickles would be placed in a boiling bath to allow the jars to seal.

After a couple of hours, Grandpa and the boys returned from the field, each laden with a five-gallon bucket of cucumbers.

"Well, Liz, we found some pretty number ones for your pickles. The boys all picked good even though we didn't have any nickels for them to find," he laughed.

"That's good, Alex. We're all ready to git started."

Grandpa and the boys left the ladies to their work. There was still a lot of fieldwork to be done. Today the tobacco had to be topped out and suckered. Topping tobacco required that you just walk down the tobacco rows and break off the top of the plant. To sucker tobacco was a little more complicated. You had to search between each leaf and look for sprouts that were beginning to grow on the main plant. This took a little longer, but in order to have a good crop, it had to be done.

Each looked for his gloves, or in the smaller boys' case, a pair of socks to be worn on their hands. A tobacco plant was covered in what is called gum, and it would stain your hands. It was also difficult to remove. After adorning their gear, they went to the field to work for a couple of hours until dinnertime.

"Grace, you go on inside and get dinner ready. Fry them two chickens that I killed and cleaned this morning. You can cook rice on the giblets and cook the butter beans that I have sitting on the table. I made up two pans of biscuits this morning, and they are sitting inside the cupboard."

"I'm going, Momma. Need anything else?"

"No, Ivory and I can manage until later on."

Grace went inside to clean and cut up the chickens. She loved fried chicken but didn't like the preparations for that particular meal. She would have to cut up the chickens, clean the gizzard, and separate the liver and heart as they would be used to season the rice. The aforementioned insides were called the giblets and did improve the flavor of rice or other things considerably.

While Grace was inside, Grandma and Ivory were washing the cucumbers. Later when they were all clean as could be, they would be placed in the largest tub, used for family bathing, and allowed to sit in a combination of lime and water for twenty-four hours. After that time, they would be sliced, some cubed, and some left whole and packed into the clean jars. The last step was to add a mixture of vinegar, sugar, and pickling spice that had been set to boil in one washpot. Finally, they would be placed into another boiling washpot and allowed to boil in the jars for fifteen minutes. This would allow them to seal, and they would then be stored away for the winter months. Pickles were used both as a food additive and could also relieve a stomach and other minor digestive problems. With the pickles out of the way, the rest of the garden would be gathered and stored for the winter months. There would be no fear of hunger and never had been for the family, for Grandma was a woman who looked well to the needs of her household, as she had been taught by her Bible, which never left her bedside.

CHAPTER FIVE

Putting in Tobacco and Picking Cotton

It was the last week of July, and the tobacco was ready for harvest. The family was excited because it was a good crop, and God willing, the weather would cooperate and allow them to complete the harvest without the bad weather that sometimes destroyed the entire crop. A hailstorm could level the plants to the ground, and the money that was needed to survive the winter would be lost. Sometimes, an early hurricane could also destroy the plants. Grandma prayed that this year would be a good one. She knew that they were in debt from last year and needed a good crop to pay off the debt and allow them enough money for the winter months and a fresh start next spring. Grandma was a special woman and knew that prayers always made the difference in any situation, whether good or bad; faith in God always paid off.

Early on Monday morning, right after the last Sunday in July, Grandpa got the barn ready to put in tobacco. The rafters had to be checked to make sure that they would hold the loaded sticks of tobacco. The heaters had to be cleaned out and filled with kerosene. The sticks were checked and stacked neatly in the holder. Spools of twine had been ordered in the spring and were ready to be used to string up the tobacco. Grandpa was lucky; he had two crates and would use his mule, along with Mr. Charlie Locklear's, as they worked together to get in their crops. He made sure the crates were in good shape and would last for the entire harvest. Ole Logan had been resting up for a week and would be in good shape to pull a crate loaded with tobacco, which would be cropped by the boys. Grandma, Ms.

Locklear, her four girls, along with Mrs. Trudy Oxendine, a widow, her daughter Sarah, and Grace and Ivory would string the tobacco.

Now the way tobacco was harvested was like this: The boys would go into the field and pick, or crop, the bottom leaves from the plant. They would then stack them neatly in two rows, opposite each other inside the tobacco crate. When the crate was full, the mules would pull it to the barn. At the barn, one of the boys usually unloaded the crate and placed the tobacco on a shelf under the barn shelter on both sides of the "stringer." Each stringer would have two people, usually girls and small boys, that would hand the leaves to them as they intertwined the tobacco and loaded it onto a tobacco stick. As each stick was loaded with tobacco, the twine was snapped and wrapped around the end of the tobacco stick to prevent it from falling off. The stick was removed by one of the "handers" and carried to the barn door. The sticks were hung up in the barn beginning at the top and continued until all the rows were full. The process of filling a barn with tobacco usually took about eight hours, which was a full day. It was hard work, but it was fun. There was a lot of knowledge to be gained by listening to the ladies talk. You always found out who was "in the family way" or who had disgraced the family in some other way.

This particular year would be the first time that Larry had worked at the barn. His job was to hand leaves to Grandma, and he was looking forward to it. He was proud of his momma and knew that she could string as fast as lightning. He also knew that he would have to work very hard. He wanted to make her proud of him and did not want to slow her down any. Grandma had practiced with him a little when she had extra time during the spring and early days of summer. She wanted her favorite boy to learn how to work well. She also knew how tender his little heart was and didn't want him to get his feelings hurt. She would never have said anything to hurt them, but she knew that if he felt that he wasn't as fast as everybody else, he would be miserable. She had devised a plan with Ms. Lowry and the older girls who would also string that day. She told them to make sure that they slowed down a little bit so that she would always finish her stick first. That way, she could train her son and spare his feelings as well. He would be a success in his first day and from then on would not lack any confidence in his ability to do a good job. She had used this method on all of the children, and it worked. She was a little nervous about Larry. He was so perceptive that if it was not carefully done, he would know; and instead of confidence, he would feel like a "baby," which he would hate. "Lord, please help me teach my boy to work hard and feel like a man," she silently prayed. After the quick prayer, a warm feeling filled her soul, and she knew that everything would be all right. Grandma smiled at Larry as he began to gather the leaves together and hand them to her to string onto her stick. His green eyes sparkled, and his winning grin went straight to her heart. She mentally thanked the Lord for the boy as the day's work began.

Larry worked hard to keep up with Grandma. He watched the other "handers" and tried to hand as fast as they did. Grandma made sure that her usual pace was a little slower. The morning flew by, and soon it was break time. The croppers came in from the field and helped with the last crate load of tobacco. Some of the older boys knew how to string, and the others handed. In no time at all, the crate was empty, and everybody could rest for about half an hour.

All of the women had brought the midmorning snack for their own families. Most had brought biscuits filled with molasses syrup or some type of meat. Grandma had flour bread with cured ham slices. She knew that Grandpa loved flour bread and liked to have meat at every meal including snack times. This was okay with the rest of the family, especially Larry. Ham was very good especially when you were extra hungry from working all morning. Everyone sat around the barn for a few minutes to eat, talk, and rest. Soon the little boys began to play a game of hide-and-seek while the older girls got ready to go home in order to prepare dinner for the family and the helpers.

It was a custom for the family whose crop was being harvested to feed everyone. This was a system that was very beneficial since no one would have to travel to their own homes or go through the extra work to bring a lunch. Everyone could go to the house, eat a hot dinner, and then have time to rest for an hour before beginning the afternoon's work.

Pretty soon, break was over; the croppers returned to the field, and those who were at the barn had a little more time until another filled crate arrived. It would be only two more hours of work, and dinner would be ready. Larry felt that the day was going by fast. He also had the feeling that only comes with the knowledge brought on by hard work. He ran up to Grandma and grabbed her around the waist. No words were spoken as she patted his curly head, but the look of love that passed between them surpassed any words that could have been uttered by even the most eloquent orator on earth. It was going to be a good harvest, and Larry was going to be a hard worker.

Tobacco season seemed to fly by. Every day there was work to do on somebody's farm, so Larry got plenty of training. By the end of the second week, Grandma was still the fastest stringer, and Larry never knew her secret method of training. He just felt like he was a good hander, which had helped his mother continue to be the best stringer. He was never to learn her secret until a few years later when, as a big boy, he watched her train his baby brother, Nelson. He then had a greater appreciation for the wonderful woman that she was and would someday use that same knowledge to teach his own children the honor that only comes with the satisfaction of a job well done.

Tobacco season soon ended although there was always something to do. If you didn't put in tobacco due to rain, you were always inside the packhouse grading and tying it up into the burlap sheets to get it ready for the market. Each day found the family on a different farm, for there were three families that worked together to get the crop in. In the evenings, just before suppertime, Grandpa and the older boys would empty the barns and take the cured tobacco off the sticks while Grandma and the girls would work in the garden and get supper ready.

On grading days, you had to sort the tobacco according to the quality of the leaf. On market days, Ole Logan would be loaded up, and Grandpa would go to the tobacco market to sell the tobacco. The price would always depend on the quality of the leaf. Grandma knew that this would be a good year, in fact the best one that they had had since they were married. She had worried all winter due to last year's harvest, which had been poor because of bad weather. She knew that they would be able to pay off their debts and put money aside for the winter. It was a good feeling.

Pretty soon, the leaves began to change, and Larry's favorite season arrived, fall. He awoke every morning to the coolness of the little boys' bedroom. Summertime was fun, but it was mighty hot. Many nights the boys had gone outside and slept on the back porch because it was too hot to sleep inside. Other nights they had gone to the river and swam. The Lumbee River was very cold, and after swimming, you usually kept cool long enough to get a good night's sleep, for toward the morning hours, the temperature always cooled down. But Larry was still glad that fall had come, for after they picked cotton, he would get to go to school.

During the month of September, the tobacco was finished, cured, graded, and sold for a good price. It was time to check the cotton sacks and make any needed repairs before the time to pick. Larry's sack was the same size as the others except Grandma sewed a double seam right through the middle of the sack. He was a small child and could only pick so much due to the weight of the cotton. He would again be taught to work and retain his dignity, for he would be able to fill up his sack along with the rest of the pickers.

One day, on the second week in October, Grandpa announced that the cotton was ready to be picked.

"Larry, son, you know you'll have to pick hard this year. We won't be able to trade work like we did with the tobacco, son."

"Why not, Daddy?" Larry asked. "Because everybody's cotton gets ready at the same time. Winter is coming on real soon and we have to get it picked as quick as we can, or we could lose the crop. It's hurricane season, and you never know when one will hit and destroy the cotton," Grandpa answered.

"Daddy, have I ever seen a hurricane?" asked the inquisitive child.

"No, son, we had some bad rains two years ago. Your momma said that the good Lord spared us. I guess she was right."

"Well, Daddy," Larry responded, "I reckon he'll spare us again this year with all the praying that Momma does." Grandpa smiled as the child went outside to play on the tree swing. Larry always amazed him with his intelligent answers. He was always careful to talk to the boy just like he was a man, and it had indeed made a difference. It had taken Grandpa raising a few boys to learn this lesson.

The following Monday, the family began to pick the cotton. It was a tedious job, but it had to be done. Grandma made sure that she had pennies to place in several places on the rows—they were so long. She couldn't afford to use the nickels, but pennies do add up and made the job a little bit more endurable. It was Larry's first time picking, and he was dead tired by the morning break. His back was killing him, and he wished that he had never seen a cotton field. He would never complain, but as Grandma picked beside him, she could read every expression.

There was no way to make picking cotton fun; it was hard work and just had to be done, but Grandma did her best.

"Son, if you want to go empty when your sack is half-full, I'll go with you," she said. "My back is beginning to hurt a little."

"I don't need to, Momma," said Larry bravely, "but I'll walk with you if you want me to, and you can tell me what school will be like." This would be his first year at school. He already knew his letters and could read. He was also good in math. In fact Grandma was afraid that he would be bored during the first part. He would be starting a little late, but so would most of the school. All of the families farmed, and the children did not go to school until the crops were all in.

"I will, son, it'll make the walk shorter if I've got you to talk to along the way." Larry felt proud and picked as hard as he could. He was picking the middle between Grandma and Don and was keeping up with them just fine. His hands were beginning to get cuts from the tough bolls, but that was to be expected. He was just glad to be big enough to work in the fields like a man.

CHAPTER SIX

First Day at School

Soon cotton picking was over, and it was time to go to school. Larry was so excited, he could hardly wait. He knew that he would be able to keep up with the class as his older brothers, and especially Grace, had taught him well. He was ready. Grandpa had ordered him new overalls from Sears and Roebuck, and Grandma had made his shirts. He had two new outfits ready to go. Of course, his favorite color, green, had been one of the shirts carefully sewed by his mother. He was to wear that the first day. Only John Willie would remain home this winter to help Grandpa get the fields ready for spring planting. He had completed grammar school, and that was the end of his education. Most children hardly finished high school due to the necessity of having to remain home to work. It was a matter of survival for the families during The Depression.

Early on Monday morning, Larry awakened to the delightful smell of smoked bacon drifting into his bedroom. He jumped out of bed. Today was to be his first day of school, and he could hardly wait to get dressed. He was going to wear his new olive green gingham shirt carefully made by his mother for the special day. He was a big boy now and could dress himself. He quickly put on his shirt and pulled on his overalls and ran into the kitchen. Since the first frost hadn't come yet, he did not have to wear shoes. On the stove was a foot tub of hot water placed there by his mother for the family to wash their faces. He grabbed Grandma by the waist and hugged her tightly.

"Thanks for the shirt, Momma. It fits just right, don't it?" he asked.

"Why, son, you are a handsome sight this morning. I can hardly believe that you are old enough to go to school. It's going to be mighty lonesome without you here every day, but I can manage if you promise to study hard. You have already learned everything out of the primer books that Grace and I've been working with. You ought to be way ahead of everybody else, but don't you act like you are better than they are, you hear me?"

"I won't, Momma. I'll learn as much new stuff as I can so when I get to be a man, you won't have to work so hard. I'll be able to help you out."

Grandma smiled and patted his curly head. She was sure that he would be good at school. He was intelligent, and more than that, he loved to learn new things. It was going to be a challenge for his teacher to keep his interest.

Pretty soon, the family gathered around the breakfast table for the morning meal. Granddaddy asked John Willie to bless the food and to remember to ask a special prayer for the children who were going to school. He knew that they had already missed two whole months and wanted them to catch up with the rest of the students. As everyone bowed their heads, John said a heartfelt prayer that was sure to fly straight to heaven and God's ears. Breakfast was good and soon over. The children gathered their books, paper, pencils, and lunch buckets to begin the two-mile walk to school.

It was a beautiful morning, and Larry was full of questions. As Luke was the oldest going, most of his questions were directed at him.

"Luke, what's it going to be like?" he asked with a small tremble in his voice.

"Well, boy, when you git there, the teacher will tell you where to sit. She's going to ask you for your full name and Momma's and Daddy's names too. Make sure that you tell her Alex and Lizzie Jacobs, okay?"

"I will, Luke. How will I know where to sit?"

"She'll tell you. It's probably going to be on the front row 'cause that's where all the first-graders sit. You will have to sit with them 'cause you're in the first grade since you ain't never been to school before. You just listen to her and everything will be all right. If anybody bothers you, you come tell me at recess time and let me know, and I'll take care of them for you."

"I will, Luke, only if they're bigger than me and I can't find a stick. You know that I can fight the devil if I have to." Luke just smiled proudly at his little brother and knew that everything would be all right.

Almost too soon, the walk to school was over. There were children playing everywhere that Larry could see. They seemed to be having the most fun, and being a friendly boy, he could hardly wait to join them.

"Boy, when the bell rings, you make sure you line up to go inside. You don't want to be late on your first day, do you?" Luke told Larry.

"I'll do just like you say Luke, but I hope that I can play for a few minutes before we have to go inside," Larry responded as he ran off to find his best friend Luther.

Before he had a chance to play at all, the bell began to ring. Larry lined up with the rest of the children and got ready to go inside. He was excited to be starting the first grade and wanted to make his momma proud. He remembered to say a silent prayer that he would like his teacher and do good.

As the children walked inside, the teachers were lined up in the order of the grades that they were to teach. Larry looked for the first-grade teacher. He spotted her, and she sure was pretty. "Boy, I'm going to like school for sure," he thought to himself. He walked up to the line and followed the teacher and students to the classroom. He was not the only child starting late. Most children from the county started at the same time, when the cotton crop was finally in. When his turn came to talk to the teacher, he walked up proudly and told her his full name and that of his parents.

"Can you read any?" Ms. Branch asked.

"Yes, ma'am. I been reading for about a year with my sister and momma," he replied.

"Well, we'll have to seat you with the other first-graders until I know how well you can read, Larry. Please take your seat on the front row." Larry sat down and prepared "to git an education" as his daddy always said.

The first thing that was done in school was the teacher said the morning prayer. Next, the children cited the Pledge of Allegiance to the Flag; finally it was time to read. The books were passed out, and Larry was surprised to see the preprimer book that he had finished a year earlier at home with Grandma. He raised his hand with an anxious look on his face. That book was for babies. He could read through the primer and wanted his teacher to know that she had given him the wrong book.

"Ms. Branch?" he asked. "I already know this book. I can read everything in it. I am in the primer book and can read most of it without anybody saying the words for me. Can I please have a harder book to read?"

"Larry, you are in the first grade, and we start with the preprimer. After we finish that, we will move on to a harder book, okay?" Ms. Branch replied patiently.

"But, Teacher, why do I have to read a book that I already can read?" he persisted.

"Because that's how we do things in school." Ms. Branch was beginning to lose her patience with the determined little child. She was not about to change her way of teaching on the advice of a mere five-year-old. She always went by the rules and wasn't about to change.

Larry was determined not to read that baby book. He tried again to get her attention, but she just went on with class. He slowly began to get mad. He had come to school to learn things that he didn't know already and wasn't about to read a book that he knew by heart.

"Teacher?" he asked again. "Can I please have another book. I done told you that I know every word in that book."

"No, Larry, you will just have to take your turn reading like everybody else."

By this time, Larry was fuming. "Ain't no way I'm going to read that baby book. Momma already taught me that," he thought to himself. He folded his arms and held down his head to try to get his temper under control. It would not do to have a bad first day. He tried but could not make it. When it came his turn to read, he jumped up furiously and again told the teacher that he knew that book. "Ma'am, I come to school to git an education of things that I don't know. I ain't going to read that book, and I already know it," he exploded. Ms. Branch was shocked and asked Larry to stand in the corner. Well, this was too much for the child. He jumped up and threw the book at the teacher and ran outside to go home.

As he ran down the road, he began to cry with terrible gulping sounds. He felt that he had failed his daddy who wanted him to learn all that he could. How in the world could he do that if they were only going to teach him things that he already knew. When he began to get near the house, he slowed down and began to think that he might just get into trouble with Momma. Well, he'd just have to, but he had a feeling that she would understand. He wasn't so sure about Grandpa though. He just might get a whipping for throwing a book at the teacher and leaving school without permission.

Grandma was standing at the kitchen window when she saw her boy walking at a slow pace down the road. Grandpa and John were in the fields, picking the cotton leavings. She walked outside on the back porch and waited for Larry, who began a very slow ascent up the steps. She saw that he had been crying and sat down on the porch swing and opened her arms. He ran into them and began wailing. It was some time before she could find out what was wrong, but between the sobs, she was able to find out why his grief was so terrible. She rocked him for a while before she spoke.

"Son, it was a bad thing to throw a book at your teacher. Your daddy will tear you up when he gets here, I'm afraid, and I can't help you this time because you were wrong.

"The best thing you could have done was stay at school all day, listen, and do what the teacher said, and then when you came home, we could have talked about it and figured out a way to help you. Since you let that temper get the best of you, you're going to have to suffer the consequences. You know how your daddy is. You have to mind your elders even if you don't always agree with them." Larry listened to his mother and knew that she was right. He also knew that he was right. There was no reason or sense in someone trying to make you learn what you already knew, and he was just going to have to take a whipping for it, although he wasn't looking forward to it. Grandpa could have a heavy hand when it came to the strap, and depending on the crime, his hand could be even heavier. Larry knew instinctively that his crime was bad. Nobody in the family had dared to throw a book at anyone, much less a teacher.

Grandma got up to go back inside and finish preparing the noonday meal. Pretty soon, Larry could hear the clop of Ole Logan's feet as he dragged the cotton wagon to the house. Grandpa and John had been picking the "scattered cotton" that had opened late. As he saw them, he mentally prepared himself to face Grandpa and take his punishment like a man. It was harder because his momma couldn't put in a good word for him. He quickly began to think of what he was going to say and frankly admitted that the truth was his best bet. He wanted an education and was going to get one, even if he had to stay home with Grandma and Grace and let them teach him. At least that way, he was always sure to learn something new. He would miss the fun and opportunity of going to school, but he was willing to risk it because he wanted to learn so bad. He wasn't going to let nothing stand in his way, not a teacher or a whipping.

As Grandpa neared the house, Larry went to the top step and sat down and waited for the confrontation. Grandpa was surprised to see the child and thought that he had gotten sick. His eyes were puffy and red.

"Son, what you doing home so soon?" he asked in a concerned voice.

"Daddy, I done something bad at school today," he quietly answered. John Willie looked at Larry and walked inside. He would get the story from Grandma, and he sure didn't want to be outside if Larry got a whipping.

"What's Lay doing home, Momma? I know school ain't out yet, not even for dinner," asked John as he walked inside. Grandma was standing at the stove with a somber look on her face. He'd seen that look plenty of times and knew that she didn't feel like talking. He quickly decided that now wasn't a good time to ask any questions, so he busied himself with washing up in the foot tub on the edge of the table. He would find out later, he thought to himself, as he went to the front room to rest a while before dinner. He was sure Lay was in some kind of trouble but knew from experience that there wasn't anything he could do to help him right now; though later on, he would be around to help comfort him.

The boy always was getting into something. He just hoped that this time, it wasn't too bad. He remembered well the whippings that Grandpa had given him in his early years, and although they weren't many, the memory remained just as poignant as if it had just happened. John was looking forward to having his own children, but he wasn't sure how he would handle it when it came time to punish them.

Outside, Grandpa and Larry were sitting on the steps. Larry had just finished his explanation of why he had thrown the book at his teacher on his first day at school. Grandpa looked at his son gravely as he cleared this throat to speak. Larry knew he was in deep trouble from the way his daddy was looking at him. Now that the telling part was over, he felt a little better, but he knew what was to come, and he waited patiently for it.

"Son, you know how much me and your momma value an education and how hard we work so you young 'uns can go to school. Me and John's been in the cotton field all morning finishing up the crop. That money's for y'all to have new shoes to wear this winter. Boy, I work too hard for you to come home and tell me something like this on the first day of school. Now, you tell me what I need to do about you." Grandpa spoke quietly.

"Daddy, you know you got to whip me for what I done. I liked the teacher, and I lost my temper 'cause she wouldn't listen to what I had to say, so I just threw that book at her and ran off. I could probably have told her again at dinnertime, and maybe she would have listened to me then. You just go on ahead and whip me like you supposed to do. I know it will be a bad one, but I'm willing to take my medicine like a man," spoke the child, showing courage that was slowly wavering.

Grandpa took Larry by the hand, stood up, and began to walk slowly toward the packhouse where he kept his leather strap. He didn't want to show it, but he hated to whip the child. He really did understand but could not condone what the boy had done. He had a responsibility to raise the child right and was going to do it no matter how much it hurt sometimes. They seemed to reach the packhouse in an instant, and Larry's bottom lip was beginning to quiver. He didn't mind the actual whipping. What really bothered him was that his father would have to punish him for doing something that was wrong, and he had known it was wrong. He had let his temper control him again.

Grandpa walked up the steps leading Larry with a heavy heart. They walked inside toward the back wall. There hung the strap in its usual place on the wall. There was a chair placed by the open window facing away from the house. Grandpa picked up the strap and sat down in the chair. Larry walked up to him and laid himself across his lap. "Boy, how many did you get the last time I whipped you?" asked Grandpa. Larry knew that his daddy knew exactly how many licks he had received, so he dared not lie. "You had to give me seven the last time, Daddy," he answered quietly. "You know what that means don't you, son?" "Yes, sir. I get ten now 'cause we always add three to it, 'cause that's your favorite number, ain't it?" Larry responded.

Grandpa began to apply the strap very sharply to his son's hips. The child began to cry but not too loud. He knew his momma was not far away and she could not bear to hear her children cry. It hurt so bad it was hard not to yell out, but he managed to endure the ten lashes. By the time it was over, he was in severe pain. He knew that now he would be allowed to cry it out while Grandpa went inside. He also knew that it would be a while before he would be able to sit comfortably again. He cried and cried and finally ended up with choking sobs. He was sitting by the window, which helped a little, due to a warm fall breeze that gently blew.

Grandpa walked slowly to the pump to wash up before he went inside. He also had to compose himself, for he hated the whippings as much as his children did. His son always managed to surprise him. He was pleased with his courage and the manly way in which he had taken his punishment. He quickly washed and walked inside, where he knew that Liz was waiting to hear how her boy had done.

"How many did you have to give him, Alex?" she quietly asked just as he walked into the kitchen.

"I gave him ten of the hardest licks I have ever had to give any of my boys," Grandpa answered soberly.

"How is he?" she asked.

"He's still crying it out, but I was proud of the way he took his punishment. I'll take him back to school after dinner, and he will have to tell the teacher he's sorry. I'll tell her to give him a book that he's never read before, and if she can't do that, I'll bring him back for you to teach until this gets straightened out, Liz."

"That'll be okay. Me and Grace will teach him if we have to, but I would sure hate for him to miss the fun of going to school."

"Well, maybe it won't come to that, we'll just have to see."

As soon as Grandpa had walked into the house, John had walked out of the front door to go and check on his brother. He walked around the packhouse and stood a little distance from the open window. As soon as Lay had stopped crying, he walked inside, reached down, and picked up his little brother. He sat in an old rocker and held the boy while his body was still shaking. Neither one spoke. There was nothing to say. John had his share of whippings, and his mother had always come to him to comfort him. It was an unwritten and unspoken rule that when someone in the family had to be punished, there was always someone who came to comfort.

One time in John's case, Grandpa had to punish him when no other family member was around. To John's surprise, a few minutes later, his daddy came and held him in his arms for a long time. John still remembered the conversation.

"Daddy, I didn't think that you knew how Momma always came and held me after a whipping."

"Son, your momma and I agreed before we got married that our young 'uns would always know that we loved them no matter what they did. She told me that I would whip and she would comfort, but just in case she wasn't around, I had better comfort her children or I would have to answer to her. I had to promise her that before she ever said that she would marry me. Your momma is a lady of her word, and I have always kept mine to her." John had vowed then and there to find a woman like his momma and be a man just like his daddy.

After a short while, Larry was composed enough to go inside the house. He looked up at John with his green eyes still glistening with tears.

"John?" he asked. "Do you reckon I hurt Momma's feelings by what I did?"

"I figure that maybe she understands," responded John. "She was a girl once herself and knows how hard it is to be good all the time. She had to learn that. I know that Momma is the best woman alive, but I have heard her and Daddy talk about growing up. Momma had her share of beatings. She's always understood and made sure we knowed that we were loved no matter what we did." The answer seemed to comfort the child more than the rocking he had received in his brother's arms. He slowly nodded his head as if trying to digest all that he had heard.

"John Willie, I'm ready to go inside and eat now if your are," Larry quietly said.

"All right, we'll go and wash up at the pump so Momma won't see how hard you cried. You know how tender her heart is over you."

The boys walked outside and went to the pump to wash their faces and hands. Both had a feeling of closeness toward the other, intensified by the companionship and mutual understanding of the priceless minutes just shared. After they were clean and dry, they walked inside to eat the noonday meal with their parents. Grandma looked up when they entered the room. Larry saw her heart in her eyes and walked over to the stove where she was standing. He grabbed her around the waist and held on tight. "I'm sorry, Momma. I will try harder with my temper." Grandma hugged her son tightly and whispered, "I know that you will do your best, and that's all I expect. Now you sit down so we can eat dinner. Your daddy is taking you back to school and will have a talk with the teacher. You are expected to tell her that you are sorry and that it won't ever happen again, you hear?"

"Yes, ma'am, Momma, I will."

After dinner, Larry and Grandpa put on their caps and began the ride back to school. They dropped John off at the cotton field to continue to work on picking the remaining cotton. "Bye, Lay, you be good."

"Okay, John, I will. I won't let you down." As the wagon began its journey, Grandpa looked at his son, knowing how hard it was for him to go back to school after leaving in disgrace.

"Son, you just walk right up to the teacher and be a man and tell her that you're sorry for what you did," he said to Larry.

"I'm shamed, Daddy, but I'll do what you tell me to," he answered in a muffled voice. All too soon, the schoolhouse came into view, and Larry swallowed hard, trying to work up his nerve to do what he had to do.

Grandpa tied the horse and wagon next to the watering trough so that Logan could drink his fill. It was a hot day, and the mule would appreciate the cool water. He got down out of the wagon and held out his hand to Larry, who took it gladly. He needed all of the confidence that he could get and received it from the firm hard grip of Grandpa's brown, work-worn hand. They walked inside and quickly found Larry's classroom. Ms. Branch was sitting at her desk with a dejected look on her face. For some reason, Larry felt sorry for her. He knew that she was new and began to feel that maybe he was the cause of her sad look. Grandpa walked over to her and introduced himself. Ms. Branch looked as if she had been crying. "Miss, I reckon you remember my boy here? He's got something to say to you, don't you, son?"

"Ms. Branch," he began with his head down, "I'm sorry for what I done this morning. I got a bad temper that gets me in trouble sometimes."

"I forgive you," she quietly said. "It is my first year of teaching, and I'm afraid that I might have made a few mistakes myself today. I should have let you read to me, but with a class this size, you just can't do everything on the second day of school. I needed to get all of the new children started off on the right foot, and you kinda have to do that right off. I know that it was your first day, and I just wanted everybody that was just starting to feel like they belonged to the class. You know that half of my students started right after Labor Day? I knew that most of the students who farmed wouldn't be here until now because of having to work. I guess I was kind of nervous because it was just like the first day of school all over again."

Larry held out his hand and surprised Ms. Branch, who quickly took it into both of hers. "We can start over, can't we?" he asked.

"We sure can if you want to. Mr. Jacobs, I think we'll be just fine. I have a few minutes and can let your son read to me. I will be sure that he gets the right book this time." Alex thanked her and patted his son on the head.

"I got to go home now and help John Willie, boy. I'll see you this evening, all right?" The child's eyes shone as he looked at his teacher. Grandpa left with the knowledge that everything would be all right now.

After Grandpa walked outside, Ms. Branch picked up the reading book that she used for her second-graders. She handed it to Larry and asked him to begin to read on page 1. She was surprised at his ability to read the book almost fluently. There were very few words on the first few pages that he couldn't pronounce. After a few minutes, she asked him to put the book down. "How are you with counting?" she asked.

"Well, I can add, take away, and can figure out my tithing money for church," he answered.

"Let's walk over to the board," she said. "If you are as good in math as you are in reading, I can put you in the second grade." She walked to the chalkboard and quickly put down six problems for him to solve. Amazingly, he solved five out of the six, missing only one multiplication problem that she was sure he could have gotten right if she had allowed him to make his marks on the board. She was excited about teaching this child who was both energetic and angelic at the same time.

"Well, little man, I guess you're in the second grade." Larry smiled and grabbed her by the hand with a look of pure happiness on his face. Just at that moment, the bell sounded, signaling that dinnertime was over. It was time for the students to come back inside for the afternoon session. Ms. Branch showed Larry where to sit and gave him his books. He was a very happy little boy and could hardly wait to get home and tell his momma the good news. He knew that she would be proud of him.

Chapter Seven

Killing Hogs for the Holidays

Indian summer was over, and every morning there was a heavy frost on the ground. It was getting cold. The birds had already flown south for the winter, and almost all of the farmwork was done until the spring. It was getting close to Thanksgiving and Christmas, and that meant that soon the hogs would be killed and the meat salted and dried so that it would last until next year.

Larry was looking forward to the day the family killed hogs. That was the best fun you could have as long as Daddy didn't include his favorite sow among those destined for the knife. He was almost afraid to ask but knew that to have any peace of mind, he would have to. He finally got up the nerve one morning just before he went off to school.

"Daddy," he asked, "how many hogs are we going to kill this year?"

"Well, so you know we usually kill three, and that's enough meat to last us, but this year I'm going to kill four."

Larry felt a sickness in his stomach, certain that one of the hogs would be Souie, his favorite.

"You ain't gonna kill Souie, are you, Daddy?" he asked with eyes filling with tears. Grandpa looked at Larry and told him no, that Souie would be around for a while. She was his best breeding sow and always had healthy pigs. She had been born the runt of the litter. Alex had almost given her away, but Liz told him to keep her. They had taken care of her, and she had turned out fine.

"I'm sure glad, Daddy. I's scared to ask you, but it's all right now," Larry said with a sigh of relief.

"Oh yeah, why we killing a extra hog this year?" he asked, a little scared although Grandpa had assured him that Souie would be safe.

"Well, son, it's for John Willie," Grandpa replied.

"What in the world does John need a whole hog for?" Larry asked puzzled.

"Well," Grandpa said, "he's finally asked Eula to marry him, and she said yes. They'll get married the week before Christmas and move into the house on the McNeil farm. John's going to work that farm. We need to help him get started and have to make sure that he'll have enough food to last through the winter. He'll need that meat so that he and Eula won't have to do without anything." Larry's face fell at the news. He didn't want his big brother to live anywhere but home with him. He felt like he wanted to cry and was mad at the same time. Grandpa, noticing the look, sat down and took the boy on his knee. He remembered how his little brother, Will, whom they had named John Willie after, cried when he learned that he was getting married to Liz. He tried to explain to Larry that John was a man and it was time to start his own family.

"Besides," he added, "you'll still see him every Sunday when they come over for dinner. You'll miss him pretty bad, but I'm sure you can go and stay with him at night sometimes, after a while," said Grandpa smiling as he remembered the magic of the first few months of married life. Larry seemed to find little comfort in his words, and he climbed down to finish getting ready for school.

Grandpa wisely remained silent. He knew that it would just take time for the child to adjust, as he worshipped his older brother, who was a second father to him. As he walked away sadly, Grandpa looked thoughtful. He knew that John would be able to talk to Larry and explain it all to him. Also, it dawned on him just how much he would miss his eldest boy. He depended on him for so much, but he also counted his blessings that he had a houseful of strong sons who would each, in turn, take the place of the eldest to help him as he ran the farm and took care of his family.

One morning, about a week before Thanksgiving, Grandpa announced that the next morning, they would kill hogs. Everyone was excited, especially Larry, who knew that Souie would be safe. The family had been getting ready for almost a month. The huge knives had been sharpened and laid carefully away so that the little ones would not find them. They had to be as sharp as razors in order to do the job of cutting up the meat. The ax and hatchets were also ready. Grandpa had his ropes cut and ready to hang the hogs to drain after the necessary preparation. All of the blood had to be drained out of them, or you couldn't eat the meat. It may seem cruel to some, but the survival of the family depended on providing food for the winter months ahead.

Grandma and the girls had cleaned out the smokehouse, scrubbing down the shelves that would hold the meat. Next, they scalded them with boiling water. The shelves had to be sanitary so that the meat could be placed there and salted. The hams and shoulders would be hickory smoked, a process that took almost a month to be ready just in time for Christmas. The Thanksgiving ham would be fresh and would be boiled outside in the washpot before being baked to a golden crisp in the oven.

It was a joyous time, and everyone was looking forward to it, especially John, who would begin to prepare and provide food for his new home in which he would begin married life with his beloved Eula. The younger children would go to school until dinnertime and return home to help with the work. Larry was looking forward to tasting the first cracklings fished straight out of the washpot. They were delicious, and he knew that his mother would have an oven baked full of sweet potatoes. He was so excited that he wondered if he could sit still in school but made up his mind that he was going to. He loved school and his teacher, and there would be plenty of time to help with the hogs when he got home as the work would last until well past his normal bedtime.

At last, it was time to go home for dinner. Larry was so excited that he began to run until a sharp word from Ms. Branch brought him to a halt.

"Larry," she asked, "what in the world is your hurry today?"

"We killing hogs today, Ms. Branch. I got to hurry home to help my momma and daddy. Dey's a'countin' on me being there," he responded. Ms. Branch smiled and waved him on. Finally, it was time to have fun killing hogs.

The children arrived at home shortly after noon. The backyard was full of the neighbors who had come to help with the job of killing hogs. Grace and Ivory were both inside the kitchen preparing the meal for the help. Grandma and Grandpa were outside to supervise the process of preparing the meat for the long winter months ahead. It was Grandpa's job to make sure the hog was cleaned and cut up for the various products to be made from the meat. As I said earlier, the hogs had to be killed the previous day and hung up so that all the blood could drain from them. You had to be very careful with pork, or it wouldn't turn out right.

Grandma was in charge of the women who would make the sausage and liver pudding as well as the souse meat, made mostly from the head of the hogs. John Willie and his beloved Eula were both helping with the process. John acted like a grown man already as he worked alongside the men. They performed the task of preparing the hog for being cut up into the various parts that would be salted and laid under the constant care of Grandma, who would make sure that the salting process would be successful. If anything happened like a warm spell, the meat would not preserve properly and would be lost.

Grandpa was in charge of preparing the hams, shoulders, and ribs to be hickory smoked. This would make the meat delicious, and Little Larry was especially looking forward to sampling the very first barbecued smoked ribs that would be prepared and served for dinner exactly two weeks after the killing for Sunday dinner.

First of all, the hog had to be cleaned and scraped to remove all of the hair from it. After hanging all night, the hogs were open and placed into iron vats, which had been placed on bricks with a roaring fire built underneath that would keep the water boiling in order to soften the tough hog hair enough to be scraped off. As the vat was not large enough to cover the entire hog with boiling water, this process was performed in three steps. In the initial stage, the hog was cut up and carefully placed into the boiling vat on one side. The next step was to turn each hog on its back to allow the boiling water to soften the hairs on the back enough to loosen up, enough for the men to scrape them from the hog. The last step in the process of preparation was to place the hog on its other side and soak the skin so that the hairs could be easily removed.

When this was over with, it took four men to lift the hog and place it on the cutting table. Bruce Scott, who was especially good at cutting up meat, was ready with the butcher knife to begin the process of cutting up the hog into its various parts. But before that could begin, the hog had to be scraped, using knives and more often seals from canning jars that had been carefully saved by Grandma for this occasion. After this process, a lot of meat was trimmed from the hog before it was cut to be used by Grandma and the ladies, who would grind it up in the grinder, add various seasonings (such as sage, salt, red and black pepper), and mix it together thoroughly to make sausage that would make your mouth water just to smell it frying in the frying pans some morning. Larry loved sausage, especially with grits and eggs, and his mouth was watering just thinking of the first breakfast of the sausage from the hogs. He liked fresh sausage the best. He also liked the other kind. To make this required a process that allowed the sausage to be hung inside the smokehouse to dry, what was called curing out. It was so good that he felt two weeks would be a long time to wait for it. Grandma had, in the past, cooked fresh sausage the morning after the killing, and he dearly hoped that she would make it a tradition. Next morning, he could be pretty sure that breakfast would consist of fresh, highly seasoned sausage to have along with his grits, eggs, and flaky buttermilk biscuits.

Now when it came to killing hogs or preparing any type of food, Grandpa and Grandma both had been taught that women who were experiencing their monthly cycles should not be around the food due to the probability of its spoiling. Although Grandma and all of the ladies in the county knew of this certainly, Grandpa felt that it was his job to make sure none who were in this condition helped with the preparations. He was always afraid that something would happen to his meat before it was preserved and his family would go lacking in the winter. He had questioned Liz that morning and was assured that everything would be all right. He had known without asking, but being a careful man, he had to make sure.

Grandma smiled silently to herself as she assured him that he didn't have a thing to worry about on that accord. Grandpa sighed a sigh of relief and again thanked the Lord for blessing him with the companion of his heart. He nodded his head, confident that he had done everything in his power to make sure they had a successful hog killing. As he wondered why he was so worried, he realized for the first time perhaps that this year was different. He was not only preparing the meat to feed his family for the winter months ahead; he was also helping his eldest and dearest son, John, get his meat ready before he and Eula officially began their life together. As he looked at his son working proudly alongside him, he could not help but feel pride and contentment as a father. He felt that he had definitely prepared his son to take on the responsibility of a family. He had the assurance that comes to any parent, of having performed the most important job entrusted to mortals, of preparing the next generation to experience independence and productivity. It was going to be one of the best days that the family had ever spent together, made even more precious for this was the last hog killing that would find the Jacobs family still living under the same roof.

The task of killing the hogs was officially underway, and everyone knew what their job was and began to perform them to the utmost of their ability. Little Larry's job was to make sure that there was plenty of dry wood for the fires underneath the washpots. He loved to play with fire and was more careful than he had been a few years ago. He had been caught setting fires without the supervision of an adult and consequently had suffered punishment from Grandpa. He now knew and respected the power of fire and knew that it must be used properly in order for everyone to be safe. He quickly ran to the woodpile and separated his wood into piles to be brought to each pot as needed. He had learned that if his wood was already sorted, the pots would boil continually as was needed to make sure that the meat was properly prepared. He was as happy as the jay birds who sang in his favorite tree in the early spring months and couldn't have asked for any better job to do.

Grandpa had already organized the men for the various jobs of preparing the meat. Grandpa's brother, Will, was to head the boiling and cleaning of the hog. He was ready with his sharpened ax, knife, and short-handled hatchet to be used in the cutting up process. Grandma also had a brother named Will, a preacher, who was to get the casings ready for the sausage and liver pudding. John and Grandpa's job was to use the long-handled grinder to grind up the meat for the sausage. It was kind of dangerous having two Uncle Wills around at hog-killing time 'cause if you hollered for one to do something quickly, the other one might stop what he was doing and mess something up. You just had to mind.

Then it was time for the ladies. My grandmother always supervised every part of the preparation process left to the women. She personally seasoned the pudding and sausage to her taste, which was a perfect blending of both her and Grandpa's tastes. Her sausage recipe was coveted by all the neighboring women. She of course had shared it with them, but theirs just didn't taste the same as hers. They all wanted to see if this year, they could detect her adding anything to the meat that she hadn't told them about. Of course, she didn't. But they felt sure that she had withheld some important seasoning that she hadn't shared in her recipe. Grandma's secret was that she always tasted her food, and if she needed to add anything extra, she did it. She had learned at an early age that you always have to experiment with a recipe in order to perfect it and make it your own. The other ladies hadn't learned this vital fact yet, and some probably never would.

For some reason that Larry couldn't fathom, he didn't really like his job on this particular day because it seemed to take him away from the excitement that was going on all around, but soon figured out that if he would stack his wood neatly in several piles nearby, he wouldn't miss much. Larry ran to and from the woodpile, bringing as much wood as he could carry at one time. After several trips, he had enough to last for several hours. Now he was free to enjoy the fun. And it was really just beginning. The pots were all boiling nicely; the men, led by Grandpa, were beginning to cup up the meat; and Grandma and the ladies were just beginning to get the parts ready to grind up for the sage sausage.

Over by the side of the yard was a huge washpot that Grandpa said could hold a week's worth of the ladies' bloomers. Aunt Marge was heading the group that would make the liver pudding and souse meat. First, the livers and other innards had to be cleaned thoroughly. Next, they would be placed into the boiling water along with onions, sage, salt, and pepper, both red and black, and boiled down to make the gravy. After that, they would be placed in the meat grinder. The last step would be to add some more seasonings and the stone-ground cornmeal. This would be mixed thoroughly and placed into the packer. At the opening, a casing would be placed there to load the pudding into, and then they were hung up in the smokehouse. Most, however, would be packed carefully into mason jars and stored in the smokehouse. This would preserve it until next hog-killing time.

Larry ran from group to group, although he constantly checked the wood on his fires, for it wouldn't do to let one burn down too low. This could cause the work to slow down. He had plenty of time to see everything, sample the meat, and keep his fires going. He liked to be big enough to help out and felt that he was in some way contributing by helping his big brother John get ready for his marriage. He felt a sense of pride in his work, yet the sadness had not yet left him. Looking over at John, filled with pride, he felt such a sense of loss, but was happy that his brother had that special grown-up look about him. He wanted to be just like John when he grew up, but he, even at such a young age, knew that he would be filling a big shoe. It was something to look forward to.

As the day progressed, the meat was almost all prepared for the winter. At dinnertime, they all ate outside in the crisp wintery air. It was the best meal that Larry had tasted in a long time. Fresh collards, fried tenderloin, cornbread, a chicken bog cooked in a washpot, and gallons of tea and cinnamon water for the young ones. There was certainly a feeling of Christmas in the air. All of a sudden, small snowflakes began to fall, which added to the excitement of the festive day. All of the children could hardly keep still. Snow was rare in Robeson County, and even the adults couldn't help enjoying experiencing the beauty.

"Look, Momma, it's snowin'," Larry called out in his excitement.

"I see it, son. Better enjoy it while you can. You know that it probably won't stick, but it sure is pretty coming down," answered Grandma. "You better keep up with your wood though," she added with a smile. Larry grinned and went to check on his pots.

It was finally time for his favorite part of the hog killing. Grandma was just about to start cooking the cracklings, which were small pieces of the skin off the hogs. They would be placed in the washpot, cooked up brown and crispy, and placed in lard cans to keep them throughout the long months ahead. Larry loved eating cracklings and baked sweet potatoes in the wintertime. It was so good coming home in the afternoons from school, smelling the odor of fresh sweet potatoes baking in the oven. Later the cracklings would be placed on a pan and baked right alongside of the potatoes until both were ready for eating. It was another one of his favorite meals in the whole world.

Cooking the cracklings took special care. You could not cook them too fast, or they would burn. The fire around the huge washpot had to burn low and constant for them to turn out right. Larry made sure that there was plenty of wood just within easy reach of the pot. He didn't want to miss a thing. The small cut-up pieces of skin were all put into the pot. Grandpa had to cut a special stick from the woods just to stir the pot with. He would walk down to where the spring ran through the woods and find a bay tree from which he would cut a limb about three feet long. He would then remove all of the bark from the limb, and it would be ready. This would add that special flavor to the cracklings and the lard and ensure that they would remain fresh until used.

Larry watched the pot excitedly and waited for the first cracklings to puff up to a golden brown. Grandma always made sure that whoever was standing closest to the pot would get to sample the cracklings, just to see if they were good. They always were.

"Boy," she said to Larry, "go and get that tin pan right over there on the table and bring it here. I'll let you taste one, and you tell me how it is, all right?"

"Yes, ma'am, Momma," replied Larry gleefully as he ran over to grab the pan. Walking back to the fire, he held the pan out with a smile of expectation on his little face. His green eyes were lit up with delight. Grandma carefully lifted out about three cracklings and put them into his pan.

"Now you better blow on them," she counseled wisely, not wanting him to burn his mouth in his excitement.

Larry held the pan close to his mouth and blew on them for all he was worth. He wanted them to cool down quickly so he could eat them. After a short while, he carefully touched one with his finger. It sure felt cool enough to eat, and sure enough it was. He had never tasted anything so good.

"Momma, them's the best cracklings you ever made!" he told her with a smile on his face.

"I'm glad you like them, son. You sure they're fit to eat?"

"They are fit enough for a king," Larry responded.

Grandma smiled and continued with the job. Soon the cracklings were ready to take out of the pot and put into the large lard cans and placed into the smokehouse for the winter. Later, when the lard had cooled, it too would be poured into lard cans to be used for making biscuits and frying various meats. Grandma also had a small pan full for Larry to take inside. She had surprised him by having Grace bake an oven full of sweet potatoes for supper. As Larry walked to the house with the pan, he thought that his mother was the best in the whole world. Who would have thought that she would've had time to think of making sure he had his favorite meal? Just her, that's all. Man, it had been the best day ever! So good, in fact, that he hadn't thought of missing out of school one time.

Another thing that he hadn't thought of, until that moment, was that this would be the last hog killing with his big brother still living at home. Soon John would be married and living with Eula right over on the next farm. His food as well as the family's would be packed carefully in the smokehouse until he was ready to move it to the house that he was fixing up for Eula. Larry felt a special pride in being able to help in some way, and he was also feeling better about his brother getting married, but not much. He would still miss him an awful lot. But as Grandpa said, "That was just part of growing up," and he desperately wanted to grow up so that he could help his momma so she wouldn't have to work so hard. It was to be a long time before he would realize his dream, and the realization of that dream was to be one of his defining moments—the one that would make him into the man he would someday be.

—

CHAPTER EIGHT

Almost Christmas

The weather was getting colder each day, which was a sure sign that it was almost Christmas. Larry could hardly wait for the day that "Sandy Clause" would arrive. It was surely the best time of the year. But before he could really plan for Christmas, John Willie was to be married the week before. Grandpa had been helping him fix up his place and get everything ready to move in. The front porch had to be repaired, as well as some the inside of the house. It was not exactly well-made, which would mean that it would be cold without some work done to it. Inside the main room or front room, John and Grandpa were repairing cracks around the windows as well as adding some slabs to the walls, which would make it warmer. John's special pride was an iron stove for the kitchen. This would serve as a stove to prepare meals on as well as heat the large kitchen and adjoining bedroom, which was to be his and Eula's. Grandma had insisted on giving this as a wedding gift. She didn't listen to any of his comments about it being too expensive. She simply told him that she wanted him to be both well-fed and especially warm. She and Eula's parents had split the cost, making it affordable for both. After a week of hard work, the house was finally ready. Eula and her sisters had tied rugs together to serve as floor coverings. They were made from strips of material that had been torn and tied together. The girls then used a large hook and made them into beautiful rugs.

They didn't have much furniture to get started with, but they did have enough and knew that if they worked together, by the time they had their first child, they would have everything that they needed. John planned to surprise Eula with the cradle that he had made in his spare time. It was beautiful, hand-carved and decorated with intricate designs, meticulously done with his pearl-handled knife. Grandma and Mrs. Sampson, Eula's ma, had sewed curtains for the living room and kitchen. Eula had made curtains for the bedrooms. Everything was colorful and inviting.

On the Saturday night before the wedding, all was ready. The food had been carefully stored in the refortified smokehouse, the heater moved in and ready for the first fire, which Grandpa would make just before their arrival to their new home. Both he and Grandma wanted the house to be warm to welcome the newlyweds home. Grace had their first supper almost ready. Grandpa was to take it when he went over to light the heater. He did plan on attending the ceremony but would leave early enough to prepare things for his son and his bride. Grace had cooked a pot of beans with salted ham, rice, and a fresh young pullet smothered in gravy. Grandpa had a pan of biscuits ready to be placed in the oven by Eula. Ivory had made a small pitcher of tea and some teacakes, which John loved. Finally, it was time to go to bed and get ready for Sunday, the day everyone anticipated.

Something was wrong with John Willie. Larry heard him pacing up and down inside the living room. He also thought he heard him crying, but that was silly because grown men don't cry, or so he always thought.

He wanted to get up and see what was wrong, but he heard Grandma's soft voice, saying, "Alex, you better go in there and talk to that boy. You remember how you felt before we got married, don't you?"

"Lizzie, that was one night I will never forget as long as I live."

"What was the problem, Alex, you have never told me in all of our years together," Grandma asked quietly.

"Liz, I's scared to death that maybe you would change your mind at the last minute. I didn't figure that I deserved you and maybe something would happen and you wouldn't marry me. I's scared too of leaving Ma and Pa and trying to make it on my own taking care of my own family. I just didn't figure that I could do a good enough job for you to chance your future on me."

Grandma laughed softly. "Alex, did you think of how much I loved you and how scared I was that night as well. I wanted to be the perfect wife and mother, but I was only sixteen as you remember. I was just a girl about to become a woman. I knew that I had a good man, but I was still afraid. Go on and talk to John, and you hold him if he needs it. He's still our boy no matter how old he is."

Grandpa got up and walked into the living room. He immediately saw the look of terror on John's face. He looked just like he did when he was a small boy. Grandpa had to turn his head away just for a second so that John wouldn't see the tears forming in his eyes. God, he loved that child. How could he let him go? Grandpa quickly composed himself and went over to where John was standing by the fireplace.

"Son, let's sit a minute," he said.

John looked both shamed and gladdened at the same time to see Grandpa. "All right, Daddy. How in the world did you know that I needed to talk to you tonight?"

"Boy, do you reckon that I've ever forgot how I felt before I married your momma?"

"No, sir, I don't guess you ever forget a thing like this. I'm scared to death, Daddy. I just hope that I'm doing the right thing."

"Son, let me tell you something that might just help you. All men feel the same way before they marry a good woman. You feel like you ain't good enough for her. You are scared about the wedding night and especially about looking after a family. Now that's a big responsibility, and you are right to think some more about it.

"Now here's the thing for you to do. First of all, have you prayed about Eula, if she is the woman who will love you for all of your life?"

"Yes, sir, Daddy. I got my answer a long time ago," John responded with a certainty that he did not show.

"Well, son, that's all you really needed to hear and that being from the Lord hisself that you had made the right choice. Everything else will somehow work itself out." Now John and Grandpa hadn't had the "talk" yet about marital relations, and Grandpa wasn't looking forward to it, but he knew that it had to be done right now.

"Son," he said, clearing his throat softly, "one thing you need to remember about women is that you have to always treat them as if they'll break. They are not like us but need to be treated real gentle like, sorta like you touch a newborn calf for the first time. For a woman, it'll be rough and hurt bad the first time, and it may not be tonight that she's ready for you. It may take weeks or months, but you be patient, and when she's ready, she'll let you know. It's not like the mating of animals but something more precious, but it has to be done in the right way and at the right time."

Grandpa's voice got a little gruff here. It sure was hard having this talk, but he knew that John needed it. After years of being a loving husband to Grandma, he felt that he had enough experience to tackle this weighty subject. He knew that his son was still a virgin with no experience with women. Eula had been his first and only love since he had first met her at a church social at the tender age of twelve.

John needed all the help that he could get. He just didn't know enough right now to ask questions, which was just as well as Grandpa covered the subject with unusual tack and thoughtfulness. John was glad when it was over and more than ready to go to bed. He felt that tomorrow would never come but knew that it would. Finally the talk was over with, and John really felt better. He also felt that he was not nearly good enough for his beloved Eula but resolved in his heart that he would be the best husband and father that he knew how to be. His daddy had taught him that. He was glad when Grandpa left his room as he had a lot to think over, and he knew that this was his last night as the eldest son in his father's house. It was hard to sleep, but John finally fell into a fitful sleep full of anticipation for the day to come, and after that, the wedding night.

Meanwhile, Little Larry spent a very restless night. He would miss his eldest brother but was looking forward to having a special place to visit. He truly loved John with all of his heart and would spend as much time as possible with him. Grandma had told him that it might be a while before he could visit, but he was content to wait. He loved his brother that much. Waiting would not be the problem, but patience, as usual, would be. He finally fell asleep but was troubled with dreams of not finding John all night.

CHAPTER NINE

The First Wedding and Separation

It was a spectacular day in December. The air was very crisp and the sunshine was as bright as it could possibly be. Little Larry woke up very early and suddenly remembered that today, John was getting married and leaving home for good. For a while, he could scarcely believe it, but soon it sunk in, and he was both happy and sad at the same time. He certainly was looking forward to all of the wedding food and festivities, but his heart suddenly sank as he realized how much he would miss his eldest brother, who was like a father to him. He looked around and decided that he would make the best of the day and look forward to visiting John whenever he could. He jumped out of bed, ran to the washstand, splashed his face, and quickly dried it off. From the kitchen came smells that he knew was special. Grandma was making John's favorite breakfast for the last time. Larry ran into the kitchen to find his mother cooking and wiping her eyes at the same time. It suddenly dawned on him that he was not the only one that would miss John. Grandma looked up at her son and smiled a sad smile, yet it was filled with hope and happiness. She wanted John to be successful and knew that if he was, then she had done her job right.

"Momma, everything smells so good, just like Christmas Day," said Larry. "You know how happy John will be when he gets a taste of your breakfast."

"Son, I sure hope so," said Grandma. "I just want things, this morning, to be special for him. Come here, boy, and let me hold you in my arms

—

71

for a minute," said Grandma. "I am not looking forward to the day when you leave me for that special woman who will make your life complete, but I think by that time, I can let you go with the same heart filled with love that I am letting John go with."

Larry ran into his mother's arms and hugged her very tightly, never wanting to let go. He couldn't imagine a life without her.

"Momma," he said, "let me help you fix breakfast this morning. Is there something I can do?" He looked anxiously at her.

"Sure, son, you can watch the sausage while I cook the grits. I just want them extra creamy this morning." Larry got a stool and placed it against the iron stove. With a fork in his hand, he carefully watched the sausage, turning it over and over to make sure it didn't burn. He loved to cook and helped every chance that he could since he had had that talk with his daddy so long ago it seemed. Grandma had made the biscuits earlier and was waiting to put them in the oven when Grandpa came into the kitchen.

"Morning, Liz, things sure smell good this morning. I know that boy will sure appreciate the extra effort you're putting into his breakfast. Boy, you watch that sausage good," he added to Larry. Larry just smiled. Grandpa knew Larry could cook, but he just wanted to say something to ease his nervousness.

"Where's John?" he asked.

"I heard him go outside early this morning," responded Grandma with an anxious look on her face. "He's been out there for a long time. You had better go and see if he's all right."

"I'll go right now, Liz. Now don't you worry, be more than likely he's just got the jitters. He'll be all right, but you might want to wait for a little while before you bake them biscuits. I'll be back in a few minutes."

Grandpa walked slowly to the door and turned around and looked at Grandma with that special look on his face. "Liz, I want you to know that I remember the day we got married. I was scared to death, but soon as I seen you at the church, everything was all right. John will be okay. I'll just go talk to him," he said as he opened the back door and went outside into the crisp morning.

Grandpa walked around the yard, and something caught his attention. He thought that it was the saddest sound that he had ever heard in his entire life. He heard a muffled sound just inside the barn door, and he knew that his boy was crying. As he walked inside, he beheld a pitiful sight—John was sobbing uncontrollably inside the barn with his arms wrapped around Ole Logan's neck. It took a few minutes for Grandpa to be able to go to John. He was crying inside himself, but he worked up the courage to walk inside the barn. "Son," he said, "everything will be all right. This is probably the toughest time you will ever have, but I can promise you one thing—if you get through this, the rest of the ride will be downhill." Grandpa put his arms around John and held him tight and just let him cry it out. After a few minutes, John was in control of himself and able to speak.

"Daddy, I don't know if I can make it through today. I've waited for this day for a long time to come, but I'm ashamed to say that I'm scared to death. I don't know if I'm good enough for her, and I don't want her to think she's made a mistake in picking me for a husband," said John with a pitiful look on his tired face.

"Son, we all feel that way some time or another, but you can be sure that there's no better man on earth for Eula than you. You are hardworking, honest, and will make a fine husband and father. I raised you to that and know you won't fail me." John smiled then and his burdens seemed to be lifted.

"Daddy," he said, "I promise you that I'll do my best."

"Son, that's all that God expects from us, and that's good enough for me. Now you, let's go to the pump and wash up. I'll walk on inside and tell your momma to put them biscuits in the stove. By the time you get there, breakfast will be ready. I'd hurry if I was you, you know your momma made all your favorites."

Grandpa walked with John over to the pump and quickly washed his face and hands in the icy cold water. "Burr, boy, this water sure is cold and will fix whatever ails you in a hurry."

John reached over and hugged his daddy with all of his might. Grandpa patted him on his back and turned to go inside.

"Thank you, Daddy, for all you and Momma have done for me. I'll never forget it," John said.

"Boy, it's no more than any parents do for their young 'uns, and I am proud to say that you are my eldest son and the pride of my heart. Don't ever fear, and remember that God will see you through your life, so says your momma, as long as you believe that he can do it."

"I will, Daddy," John said as he began to wash up. "I'll be in in a few minutes, okay?"

—

"All right, son, breakfast will be ready for you when you get there."

Grandpa walked inside the house and looked at Liz. He just nodded his head and said, "You go on ahead and put them biscuits in the oven, Liz. The boy's on his way." Grandma smiled and knew that everything would be all right.

Breakfast was wonderful. There were the sausages that Larry had slaved over, or so he thought, fresh ham, grits, biscuits, and for a special treat, Grandma had made the breakfast potatoes that John loved. She also has pitchers of fresh milk, preserves, and syrup. Everyone sat down, and for the last time, John was asked to bless the food for the family.

It was a beautiful and simple prayer spoken from the heart, which made the family feel special. As John humbly asked God to give him the strength to be a good husband, there were audible signs of tears from Grandma and the girls. Even Larry felt a tear spring to his eyes, but he tried to hold it back. He quietly wiped it away and figured that he could cry later if he needed to, but now it was the last breakfast that the entire family would have together, and he wasn't going to let nothing spoil it.

As the amens were said, the family began to eat. For a time, you couldn't hear nothing but the "pass me this" and "do you want another biscuit?" It was a wonderful meal, and everyone enjoyed it, but it was over too soon. The chairs were pushed back from the table, and everyone went to get ready to go to the church. The service was set for eleven o'clock, now that it got dark so early and no one wanted to be late.

John went to his room and got out his new black suit and began to get dressed. Larry followed him and noticed that John had forgotten to shine his shoes.

"John, can I shine your shoes for you?" he asked.

"Thank you, boy," said John. "I reckon I been so nervous that I plain forgot."

Larry smiled, grabbed the shoes, and ran into the kitchen to get the shoeshine box. He felt good to be able to do something for John. He got his little stool and sat beside the stove. Not a sound was heard but the shining cloth rubbing the shoes. When he finished, they looked like glass. Grandma had watched him the entire time without a comment. He had such a look of love and concentration on his face that she was afraid of spoiling it. She knew what this meant to him and was proud to be able to do this last thing for the brother that he loved and revered as a father. He had such a compassionate heart, no job ever seemed to be dull to him as long as he was helping someone else. She had seen it in action often and knew that of all her children, he was the most special to her. Larry finished the job and jumped up and ran to the boys' room, where John was putting the finishing touches on his appearance.

"John!" Larry cried. "You look like a grown man, just like a preacher or something." John smiled and rubbed the curly head, looked into those beautiful gray-green eyes and grabbed Larry and held him tight.

"Thank you, boy, and thank you for doing my shoes for me. They sure look good. I don't think I could have done better myself." Larry smiled and felt proud and happy.

"Well, I reckon I better go and get ready. I don't want to make Momma have to come and help me now that I am a big boy," he said as he walked away proudly.

Since the drive to church would take an hour, the family had to be loaded in the wagon at ten, so there wasn't a whole lot of time to waste. Everyone got ready and looked their finest. Grandpa had a surprise for Grandma. He had bought her a new store-bought dress for the wedding. He had been saving it to give it to her on this special morning. Of course, Grandma had already made a dress, which was beautiful, and she had no idea that she was to be the recipient of such a wonderful gift. Grandpa knew she would fuss, but he would just tell her it was an early Christmas present. When he entered the kitchen where Grandma was finishing up, making sure the preparations for the couple's supper was underway, she looked up as he came inside the door. He had a look on his face that she didn't see often, the look of a little boy who was extremely proud of himself and a little scared at the same time.

"Alex, is something wrong?" she asked.

"Well, no, Liz, I just wanted to give you something and tell you what a wonderful woman you are." He quietly walked over and put a package in her hands and waited for her to open it. Inside was a beautiful dress, her favorite color, blue, and the most beautiful dress she had ever seen. She was speechless and looked up with tears in her eyes. For a moment, she couldn't speak; she was so overwhelmed.

"Alex, this dress must have cost a fortune. You shouldn't have wasted that money on me."

"Liz"—Grandpa's eyes blazed—"there is no waste when you buy something for the woman you love and the mother of your children. You never asked for anything and deserve more than I can ever give you, so don't ever say that anything spent on you is a waste." Now Grandpa seldom spoke that way to Grandma, but when he did, she knew not to say anything.

"Thank you, Alex. I will wear it with pride and cherish it for the rest of my life. I'll never wear it again, but I want you to bury me in it, all right?"

"I will. If that's what you want, Liz, I'll sure do it, but I hope that that day is long in coming. I don't know what I'd do without you," Grandpa said, and he wrapped his arms around her for just a second.

"Alex, you better go and get ready, hadn't you?" she smiled. As Grandpa turned to go, he gave her such a look of love that few people ever see in their lifetime from anyone, nodded his head, and walked slowly to their room to get ready.

Grandma just looked at that dress with tears in her eyes. She had wanted a new dress but hadn't dared mention it. She silently thanked God for it and for the wonderful man who truly loved her.

The family was all ready and loaded in the wagon a few minutes before ten, everyone except Grandma. As they waited, she walked onto the porch, and the whole family looked in surprise. She was a pretty woman and was sure going to be the best-dressed one there. Larry jumped off the back of the wagon and went to help his momma into her seat. He just looked at her; she looked so fancy he was afraid to touch her. "Momma, you sure are real pretty," he said shyly. "Thank you, son," she said, pleased.

As she stepped onto her seat beside Grandpa, he just looked at her and smiled. "Woman, you look real nice," he said as he began to drive away. Grandma smiled and patted his hand.

"Thank you, husband," she said.

The family began the long drive to the church where John was to be married.

It was a quiet ride with everyone lost in his or her own thoughts. John was beginning to fidget a little, and Larry climbed in his arms, sensing that he needed someone to hold him close. As he put his arms around his brother, he felt a sense of peace and calm and suddenly knew in his heart that things were as they should be. He was ready and would never fear again.

The wagon creaked along the road slowly since it had been dry for a long time. No one wanted to get dusty, and Grandpa guided Logan with extra care. All too soon, the church rose into view, white and beautiful with the steeple gleaming in the bright sunshine. *You just couldn't go wrong if you started your new life at church* was John's last thought before they parked and got outside.

All of the neighbors had begun to arrive, and many were calling out to John as they walked up to the church. John felt really proud and was glad that they thought enough of him to come. The men were shaking his hand, and the women were patting him on the back. Every family had brought a dish, as was the custom for the meal following the wedding. The smells were wonderful, and Larry could hardly wait for the pineapple cake Momma had baked. That was his daddy's favorite cake, and his too.

Everyone walked inside except John, Grandpa, Grandma, and Luke, who was to walk her inside and seat her. The preacher came up to John and asked if he was ready. Now John hadn't seen Eula and was worried that she was late. He whispered to the preacher if she was there yet and was told yes. She was in the back so that he couldn't see her until she walked down the aisle. John breathed a sigh of relief, and they were ready to proceed inside. Luke proudly walked his mother up the aisle and seated her in her place.

Next came the preacher, Daddy, and John to take their places up front. A hush came over the church as the piano began to play. The back doors opened, and there stood Eula, all in white, on her father's arm. Everyone stood up as she began her walk up the aisle to stand beside her father, to be given in marriage to John. From the moment he saw her, John couldn't take his eyes off her. She was so beautiful, more that he could even imagine, and most importantly, she was to be his forever. It was a wonderful feeling. As she came down the aisle, she began to cry as she saw John. A lot of the women were crying as well. Larry wondered why, but soon felt a feeling in that church that he had never felt before. A feeling of magic he would later come to understand as the Spirit of God, which warms hearts and causes eyes to shed tears simply because of the magic of divine love. Grandpa felt it too, and his heart was changed in a twinkling. His eyes began to run water, and he finally understood the message that he had heard preached all of his life, that true love was when a soul believed in and accepted Christ as Lord and King. As he stood beside his son, he quietly gave his life to God. Grandma knew in an instant. She saw the change come over him, and her eyes filled with tears. This truly was a blessed day already.

The ceremony was beautiful, and there wasn't a dry eye when Eula looked at John and said with all of her heart, "I do." Many there were moved, and the older ones remembered the day when they first married. They also knew the trials that would come but felt that the couple standing before them would make it. It was a beautiful and moving ceremony. As the preacher pronounced them man and wife, everyone stood up and said, "Amen." He also invited the congregation to accept the responsibility of helping the new couple and asked loudly if they were willing to do so. And if so, to say "I do" as well. Well, the church rang with sound of *I do*'s and the couple proudly walked down the aisle as husband and wife, feeling that they could conquer the world.

The marriage supper was delicious with everything that you could imagine to eat. Even Larry, who could eat a horse, as Momma always told him, was filled to the brim. As the meal was finished, Grandpa stood up to make an announcement. First, he said how proud he was of John, and then he broke down and told them that he had gotten saved that day. It was a wonderful time, with the preacher shaking his hand and the men and women all crying and hugging him. Everyone had prayed for Grandpa, for he was such a good man; it was a waste that he wasn't in church. But all was right now. John just hugged his daddy and cried. "Daddy, you have made me more happy than when I took Eula for my wife," he said. "Thank you for making this a perfect day." Grandpa couldn't do anything but cry and hug him back.

Everyone was so excited that the dinner turned into a revival, and several more got saved that day. No one had seen anything like it before. It was seldom heard of people getting saved at weddings, but today sure was an exception. Grandma was so happy that she couldn't do anything but smile. All of her prayers were answered, and she felt that she could die happily right now and never want anything else. But then she looked at her children and never wanted to leave them alone to fend for themselves without a mother and asked God to allow her to see them grown.

The supper was over, the dishes washed and packed up, and everyone was ready to go home. John and Eula were both tired and looked it. Luke was to drive them home where the girls would have made the house ready for them. A fire would be in the stove and their supper on it. As they began to walk to the wagon, Grandpa and Grandma both walked with them. A last hug was shared, and they drove off to begin their new lives together.

Larry looked after the wagon until he could no longer see it. He felt the tears begin to well up in his eyes and felt his daddy's hand on his shoulder. "Son, it's going to be all right."

"I know, Daddy, but I'm sure gonna miss having him at home." sighed Larry sadly.

"I will too, son, my old heart aches to see him go, but I'm proud too that I have raised a man ready for life."

"Daddy, there's something I want to ask you about. What happened to you back in the church? Are you saved for real?"

"Yes, son, I'm proud and humbled to say that I am a Christian like your momma. I have never felt better in my life and wish that I hadn't waited so long 'cause I've missed so much. But one thing about it, Lay, I'll never turn back, and if I fall, I will fall into my Lord's loving arms and stay there forever." Grandpa's voice broke here, and Larry felt the power that ran through his daddy as he said those words. He also knew that heaven was a place where you wanted to go when you died and that took being a Christian. He was glad that his daddy was one now. As they stood in the churchyard, waiting for Luke to come back, the sun began to turn to a bright red, getting ready to set and bring an end to the day. They both watched the sunset together, and somehow each knew that there would be many more partings, but each one would bring a new beginning just as the sunset ended one day and began another filled with promise.

www.ingramcontent.com/pod-product-compliance
Lightning Source LLC
Chambersburg PA
CBHW021240280526
45784CB00005B/2181